B.B. King
A Life of Blues

Richard Booth

Copyright © 2015 Richard Booth
All Rights Reserved
ISBN 10: 1517115825
ISBN 13: 9781517115821

"B.B wasn't a star; he was a moon. Stars can burn out, but moons never do".

Rufus Thomas

For Maz, Matti, Sylvie, my family and B.B. King

TABLE OF CONTENTS

	Foreword by Stanley Abernathy	v
	A Message from the Author	vii
	Acknowledgments	ix
	INTRODUCTION	1
1	IN THE BEGINNING	5
2	ARRIVAL AT BEALE STREET	9
3	CREATING THE KING	17
4	THE BLUES IS DYING	24
5	KING WORLDWIDE	31
6	RETURNING HOME	38
7	MEETING B.B.KING	46
8	LATER YEARS	56
9	TWO WHITE HORSES	61
10	THE THRILL IS GONE BUT NEVER FORGOTTEN	69
11	TRIBUTES: TO B.B. WITH LOVE	73
12	AWARDS AND HONOURS	102
13	LUCILLE	111
14	DISCOGRAPHY	120
	References: Selected Bibliography	156
	Notes	158
	List of Illustrations	164
	ABOUT THE AUTHOR	181

Stanley Abernathy, B.B. King and Jesse Jackson
(Collection of Stanley Abernathy)

Foreword by Stanley Abernathy

I had the honour of being in Mr. King's band for 25 years. I can say it was a life changing event. I knew him 15 years prior to that having been in Bobby 'Blue' Bland's Band. The two bands were like family, and whenever we were on the same bill it was like 'ol home' week. I felt we got to know each other well during those times. When 'Blue' became sick and couldn't work as much, Mr. King had a Summer Tour happening where he would expand his band. I got the call to be a part of that and it was unreal and a lot of fun!

After two summers I asked Mr. King if I could stay. He gave me the okay and for the next 25 years I was part of a historic event. You get to know a person real good when you're doing 320 days a year and travelling the world.

There are a lot of stories that will stay in the Band Family. But in some 40 years I have never known a more humble and generous person in my life. He always had time to stop and ask if everything was alright. A more approachable person I've never met. I miss my friend and will never forget those lessons I learned from him. B.B. KING was the real deal and I am proud to have called him my friend.

Stanley Abernathy
August 10, 2015

Photo signed to the author from B.B.

A Message from the Author

It has been thirteen years since I first began to write this celebration of the life and work of B.B. King. Now as I write this dedication, my musical hero and friend, Riley B. King has passed away.

It is sad to think that fans will no longer have the chance to see the King of the Blues performing live. The more I think of it, I can't help but reminisce of the many times Mr. King has ventured over the water to Europe, UK and the countless shows that he has performed all over the world. No person I can think of in recent times has matched the hectic touring schedule that B.B. King placed upon himself over the years. He will continue to inspire future generations of fans all over the world.

I feel very proud that I managed to give B.B. a bound copy of this book back in 2006. It was always my intention to publish this book during his lifetime, but I cannot think of a greater tribute, now, than to publish this updated and expanded edition in memory of my friend and this great man.

Thank you Mr. B.B. King for all the years of music, shows and friendship that you have given to millions of people all over the world. This is for you - your lasting legacy and place in musical and cultural history.

Richard Booth
July 2015

Acknowledgments

I wish to thank the following people, without whom, this book would not have been possible.

A huge thank you to Mary Walker Owens of Great Sky Publishing for your friendship, editing and assistance. Without your dedication and hard work, this book would not have been possible.

To my dear wife Maz, who gave me the space to do all the hard work needed to get this book created and ready for publication.

To the amazing people who gave their time and support in providing beautiful words and photos in tribute to Mr King, especially; Stanley Abernathy, Tony Coleman, Leonard King, John Mayall, Keb Mo, Regi Richards, Rita King, Early Clover, Andrew Goodman & Pauline Lee of Getty Images, Charley Gallay, Mississippi Public Broadcasting and the B.B. King Museum and Delta Interpretive Center.

And to the great man himself, Mr. Riley B. King, The King of the Blues, B.B. – my hero, my friend, my inspiration to write these pages to pay tribute and to celebrate your amazing life and career. There are not enough pages to document your accolades, awards and what you have achieved in your lifetime. You meant so much to millions of people across the world and will continue to do so - both with your amazing legacy of music and with your place in musical and cultural history. This is for you, my dear friend, with love and appreciation.

Signed tour programme from B.B. to the author

INTRODUCTION

I have been a fan of B.B. King and his fantastic music for many, many years. His inspiring guitar playing and blues sound is still heard and loved the world over. There are many great, informative books about B.B. King, but I wish to provide my own personal account and to tie in all the facts of his long and distinguished career.

I really didn't think too long about writing a biography about B.B. King. I first had the idea at 4:50 am one rainy Monday morning during my drive to work. My friend's first novel had just been released and I was inspired to write my own book after I finished reading his that weekend. What better person for me to write a book about than my musical hero B.B. King! I was already running the UK fan club and website for B.B. and his fans. I had also read and learned so much from some amazing books about the blues great whose birth name was Riley B. King: Charles Sawyer's, 'The Arrival of B.B. King', Sebastian Danchin's 'Blues Boy: The Life and Music of B.B. King', and Joe Nazel's 'B.B. King: King of the Blues'. However, it is B.B.'s own autobiography 'Blues All Around Me' that first offered me a really frank account of his life - and a humble view at that.

I hope that this book will give readers further insight into the forever reigning 'King of the Blues' and also provide you with more information about Riley's amazing journey. I wish to thank my family and most of all, my wife for putting up with me constantly playing B.B. King music all the time! Also, for understanding when I would leave her for days at a time to follow B.B. on his tours reviewing shows for the website and fan club, experiencing the ultimate live show at various venues. B.B. King was the friendliest person you could ever wish to meet and always had time for his fans. I have had the good fortune to meet B.B. personally at many shows and hotels over the years. I also have a constantly growing B.B. memorabilia collection, along with many autographs, including a signed Gibson Lucille, which is my prized possession.

B.B. King was the hardest working artist alive and at nearly 90 years of age was still going strong. This is for you B.B., a lasting legacy to a very special man.

Richard Booth
Shropshire, June 2015

Signed photo from B.B to the author
(Collection of Richard Booth)

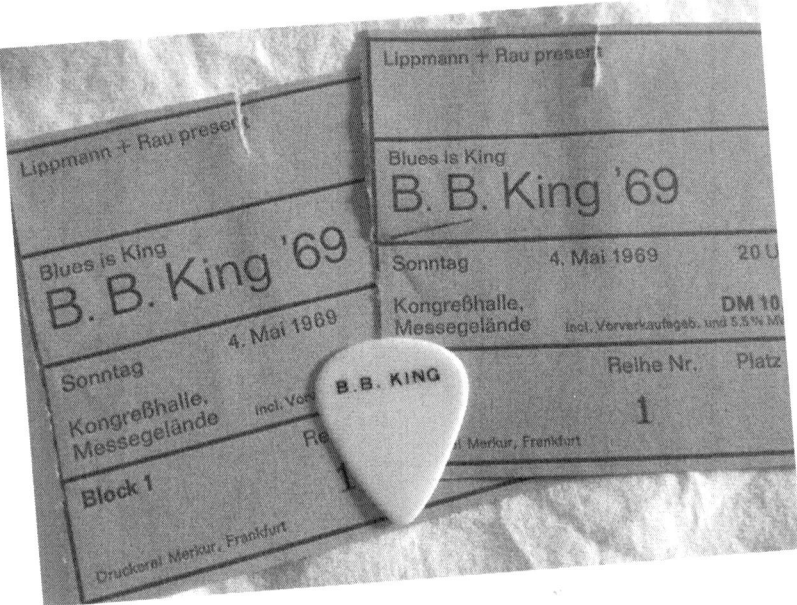

Concert tickets and guitar pick from 1969
(Collection of Richard Booth)

Photo: Charles Sawyer

IN THE BEGINNING...

> *"I remember my childhood. How things were with us then, the race problems and how bad it was in the 1930's. There were tragedies I experienced I could never talk about, so it all just stayed with me and so did the blues."* [1]

B.B. King was born Riley B. King on September 16, 1925 on the Mississippi Delta near Itta Bena, about twenty miles east of Indianola. When Riley was four years old his mother left his father, Albert King and moved to Kilmichael, where most of her family still lived, taking Riley with her. Over the next five years his mother Nora Ella and his grandmother Elnora Farr raised Riley. In 1935 when young Riley was just ten years old, his mother died. Some of the advice she gave him just before she passed away stayed with him throughout his life:

> *"Act justly and fairly in everything and at all times, without looking for anyone's approval for doing so."* [2]

That was the code Riley B. King used to follow his path throughout life and it was a very successful one. Still, as a result of the stresses of his childhood, B.B. always needed reassurance from others around him and this made him develop a stutter which he would eventually overcome.

Between the ages of 9 and 14, Riley King worked for his grandmother in the fields of Edwayne Henderson. His education was developed at Elkhorn School, where Luther Henson made a long-lasting impression on Riley. He loved music and records, especially his Aunt Mima's large collection of early 78's of that era. She had music by many recording heroes: Blind Lemon Jefferson and Lonnie Johnson amongst others. Yet it was gospel music, more than the blues, at that point in his life that helped Riley develop his musical talent.

The first electric guitar player he heard was played by a preacher named Archie Fair in the hills of Mississippi. Fair used to visit his brother-in-law and brother to Nora Ella, William Pullian. When the adults went for dinner, Archie would lay his guitar on the bed and Riley, as he later recalled, would eagerly crawl up on the bed and begin to play with it:

> "... One day he caught me and decided to show me a few chords, C, F and G. Even today I still use those same chords a lot." [3]

After his Grandmother died in 1940, Riley's father came to pick him up and moved him with him back to Lexington. It wasn't long before Riley didn't feel he belonged there and he cycled 60 miles, determined to return to Kilmichael. Upon arrival he went to see the Hendersons who were good to him. They helped arrange for him to stay with Flake Cartledge on his plantation. B.B. had now regained his gospel group, Elkhorn School, and his adopted family. Riley worked hard on the Cartledge family's farm. The days were very long. He walked the entire five miles to school and back. In the morning and every evening, he had ten cows to milk. He earned $15 a month and those memories B.B. later would say were,

> "One of the happiest parts of my life." [4]

He was also at this time trying to buy his first guitar. His boss would finally buy it for him after B.B. asked him to. He took the money back out of his wages by installments. That first guitar as B.B. fondly remembered was a red Stella with a resonator hole. A few months later, his hard-earned guitar would be stolen from his cabin on the Cartledge land. Young Riley was heartbroken and couldn't believe that someone really could steal someone else's property, especially the one thing so dear to him.

Later, Riley left Kilmichael in search of work on the Delta. His cousin Birkett helped him find new employment. He went to the Barrett plantation where Riley B. King soon proved himself to be intelligent and competent at his work. He became a good tractor driver, something he always remained very proud of. Cotton pickers were only paid between 50 cents and $1 per hundred pounds of cotton picked. A good tractor driver like Riley could make up to $5 a day. *"I was one of the top tractor drivers"*, *B.B. would later say.*[5]

On September 16, 1943 on his 18th birthday, Riley was obliged to report to the draft board. He attended basic training for three months, but wasn't sent to fight because of his status as a tractor driver. He was able to fulfil his military service obligation by working for his boss Johnson Barrett on his land. Riley also had a busy social life outside of work. On Saturday nights, he and his friends headed for clubs in Indianola to listen to music and would see some of the greats at the time in live performances at various venues. One other person was also seen often with B.B. at that time: his new girlfriend Martha Denton, who became the first Mrs. King.

Blues music was heard on the Delta radio with famous blues musicians being aired frequently. B.B. commented later on how the blues was first viewed.

> *"When the blues started, a lot of times the songs didn't really mean that the old lady left the man or the house had burnt down. It meant something far beyond that."* [6]

During that time on the Delta, Riley also discovered two important musicians who influenced his style: Django Reinhardt and Charlie Christian. He would still continue to work with his local gospel group, but one Saturday afternoon when his 'Famous St. John Gospel Singers' were unavailable, Riley decided to play on the streets of Indianola. When he came home, he had twice the money in tips than from a weeks' work on the plantation. After a few months of earning better money from playing music, he began to dream of heading south.

Riley's mind was completely made up when he broke the exhaust pipe off his tractor in an accident. He left the plantation that night as he was worried about what his boss might say. He headed off, traveling on the highway toward Memphis, with his newly replaced guitar and $2.50 in his pocket.

Beale and Second Street.

The building on the corner of these streets became
B.B. King's Blues Club

(Courtesy of Memphis and Shelby County Room,
Memphis Public Library & Information Center).

ARRIVAL AT BEALE STREET

Riley was 21 years old when he arrived in Memphis, Tennessee. He knew that his cousin Bukka White, who was popular on the blues circuit, lived there and he had to find him if he was to survive in his new surroundings. Not only was Memphis the 'Home of the Blues', but also at that time the nation's 'Murder Capital'. He went to several places, bars and clubs, to see if anyone knew Bukka. As his cousin was well known, many people knew of him but didn't actually know where he lived.

That first night in Memphis, Riley slept in the back room of a saloon, but he eventually found Bukka White after a second day of searching. Bukka would help young Riley learn more secrets of the guitar. As there were many guitarists looking for the same big break, Riley knew he had to study hard if he were to make it big.

The centre of the blues was 'Beale Street'. It was there that W.C. Handy, often referred to as 'The Father of the Blues', refined blues music and gave way for a multitude of musicians including Riley B. King, to develop their own style of playing. Riley also cited Charlie Christian, Django Reinhardt and T-Bone Walker as major influences. T-Bone Walker's playing encapsulated the instrument that would become B.B. King's rhythmic voice: the electric guitar:

> *"When I heard T-Bone Walker playing the blues on an electric guitar, that just did it all. It was like I had become of age."* [7]

B.B would also later point to Lonnie Johnson as the performer who "linked him to jazz". [8] He said that musicians respected Lonnie Johnson,

> *"... but he also had the 'know how' for mingling with the people. I like to think of myself as a Lonnie Johnson, a man without enemies."* [9]

These men would have a lasting influence on Riley's playing,

> *"Every time that I feel the need for that change in my battery again"*, B.B. explained in an interview, *'I'll put one of them on. They seem to have one thing in common, shopping for notes."* [10]

Early advert featuring B.B. King at WDIA radio

Riley's playing also improved with Bukka's help and soon he could play as well as the other blues players who packed themselves onto Beale Street or at Beale Park. However, he still thought about his responsibilities back in Indianola: his wife and the debt he owed to Johnson Barrett for the damage done to his tractor. As he was making only a little money from playing the blues at that point in time, Riley would return back to Indianola to face his problems. He settled down with Martha once again and worked hard to repay the money owed to Mr Barrett. Yet he still continued to dream of returning to Memphis and making it big on Beale Street.

Late in 1948, Riley was ready to head back to Memphis again and hit the big time. An important event would also occur that became a fundamental aspect of Riley King's early career. WDIA AM radio began introducing a black music format. So, when Riley with guitar in hand, arrived back in Memphis, he began to make real contacts.He found blues man and radio disc jockey Sonny Boy Williamson of KWEM radio in West Memphis, Arkansas, across the river from the west end of Beale Street. Riiley asked him,

> "Can I play a tune over the radio?" [11]

Sonny Boy opened his mike to Riley and asked his radio audience to call in and rate his performance. Riley received a number of calls from listeners and was hired. He would become a stand-in performer for Sonny Boy Williamson, who was overbooked. At the same time, Riley also went to work at Miss Anne's Sixteenth St. Grill in West Memphis. It was a very poorly paid position, but it was a start.

Young Riley would soon be offered a permanent job at WDIA playing and singing at $25.00 per week. On the plantation early in his life, he had been earning only 35 cents a day! Now, on the same day he visited WDIA radio, and after an unscheduled performance for an impromptu audience, Riley King had been offered a daily ten-minute radio show! The show was sponsored by a 'tonic' known as Pepticon. As the 'Pepticon Boy', Riley had to introduce the product by singing this 'persuasive' little jingle:

> "Pepticon, Pepticon, sure is good
> You can get it anywhere
> In your neighborhood" [12]

For the remainder of the ten-minute show, Riley was allowed to play anything he wished, and he soon became very popular with the listeners. As a result of this, the WDIA station manager

B.B. King's personal copy of 'Wheelin' on Beale' book from the author, Louis Canter.

hired Riley as a DJ and he began hosting the 'Sepia Swing Club' for blues listeners across Memphis. Riley now would have to change his radio name, in order to make himself a real success. After much discussion, Riley B. King became known as 'The Beale Street Blues Boy'. As this was a lot to say in one go, it was shortened to 'Blues Boy King' and later to 'B.B. King' as he is now known all over the world today.

In different neighbourhoods, Riley as 'the 'Pepticon Boy' would visit stores where the tonic was sold, singing and playing his guitar.

> "When they would sell so many, they would usually give me a bonus for going out. Sometimes I would get fifty or sixty or maybe a hundred dollars just for being out that day and that was very big money for me." [13]

B.B. also always remembered with a smile:

> "*One of the salesmen said they would listen to me because they could see I had a honest face!*" [14]

During that same period, Riley would also develop a strong love of gambling, which he continued to love during the remainder of his life. Some of his money he would win, and some he would lose, during those days as the 'Pepticon Boy', but B.B. still didn't let that get in the way of his promise to bring his wife Martha out to Memphis to be with him. He would later recall that Martha had already moved to Memphis only a week after he got his job at WDIA radio.

Riley's successful radio program would also earn him shows at all of the local blues clubs. His reputation quickly grew throughout the South as WDIA raised its wattage to 50,000. Black radio was no longer a small time event. It became hugely popular across the American landscape.

During the winter of 1949, B.B. King was also playing gigs outside of Memphis. One incident at a club in Twist, Arkansas created a real life music legend. On a cold December night, B.B. was playing a show, but it was extremely cold inside the little club. The owner had placed a cylinder half-filled with kerosene to provide some heat. Two guys started a fight, during which they knocked over the cylinder filled with the kerosene. Flames began to fill the room and everybody ran outside for their lives. B.B. got out of the club, relieved to have escaped, but then realised he had left his guitar inside!

He didn't hesitate to run back inside and rescue his beloved guitar. B.B. said of that incident:

> "*Good guitars are hard to find and I sure don't have the bread for a new one.*" [15]

Riley found his guitar just as a beam crashed down in front of him. He grabbed it and left the club just as the wall collapsed.

After the incident, B.B remembered that a patron remarked:

"You wouldn't think two guys would near kill each other over a gal like Lucille!" [16]

B.B. decided to name his instrument '*Lucille*' as he later recalled:

"If only to remind me never to do anything that foolish again!" [17]

B.B. King Gibson Lucille
(Collection of Richard Booth)

With B.B. backstage during the 2006 UK tour with my prized possession, my signed Lucille guitar.
(Collection of Richard Booth)

Very early B.B. King and his orchestra photo
(Collection of Richard Booth)

CREATING THE KING

Things were now working out well for Riley B. King. He had gained some success, but the oppressive laws of America still segregated people. This made it difficult for him to reach out to white audiences, but B.B. had made the big time and he soon developed a huge following. They went to every club he played. They listened to his radio show and broadcasts. Then, in 1949, B.B. King was offered a chance to make a record. This offer was the beginning of his historic music recording career.

B.B. had asked Bert Ferguson at WDIA, about the possibility of making a recording. Bert knew Jim Bullet who ran a recording company, so he mentioned Riley to him. B.B.'s first recordings were for Bullet Recording and Transcript Company. Four titles were recorded: 'Miss Martha King', 'When Your Baby Packs Up and Goes', 'Got The Blues', and 'Take a Swing With Me'. These songs were released in the summer of 1949 on two Bullet 78s. B.B. would also later record six singles for RPM Records. Those few early singles didn't achieve exceptional sales, but enough to generate huge interest.

While he was making records, B.B. was also becoming a major attraction at the local Chitlin' Circuit of black clubs and, at the same time, still working on radio. 'Three O Clock Blues' was the first of the long string of hits that would long sustain B.B. King as a leading African-American musician for many years. As soon as it was released (B.B.'s seventh RPM single), it brought significant attention to reviewers and DJ's all over the country. This did a lot to further the record's success. Then, a few days later, it started to sell all over the country.

Two days before New Year's, 'Three O'Clock Blues' made the Billboard Chart and became Number #1 on February 2, 1952. For B.B. King, it was the beginning of what one author later called "profound changes in his way of life and his conception of his music."[18] B.B.'s earnings also suddenly took off:

> *"I had been making about $85 a week with my playing and being on the radio and everything else I could do - $85 total and when I recorded that first big hit, I started making $2,500 a week."* [19]

Another change was for B.B. to appear in larger Black American venues. Bert Ferguson at WDIA and B.B.'s manager at the time, along with Robert Henry did their best to set this up. They decided to sign Riley to one of the best known booking agencies in the county, New York's 'Universal Attractions'. They signed him to an exclusive contract for six months. Due to being exclusive, the deal would discourage the greedy attentions of other promoters and, as it was for only six months, it also protected Universal in case B.B. King's career did not prosper.

Tiny Bradshaw's orchestra, one of the most popular bands in the early 1950's, supported B.B. on his first national tour. They undertook to play some of the more prestigious concert halls in the country. There were the large theatres and venues such as the Regal in Chicago and the Apollo in New York. These venues had both made and ended other performer's careers. A theatre like the Apollo would put on the same show about 30 times a week. At each of the five daily shows, running from noon to midnight, there would be a film, followed by various music acts. For B.B. King, this would be the test of his ability to further promote the success of 'Three O'Clock Blues'.

B.B. would become very nervous before his first show at the Howard Theatre in Washington but, after a few days, he had become at ease on stage. He won over the crowds and his first tour was a complete success. Over the next few months, B.B. would tour the biggest theatres in the South East. He still didn't quit his radio show at WIDA, though, and asked his boss to keep his place open. Bert Ferguson was only too glad to agree, as having such a famous star at his radio station could really boost its appeal.

B.B. recorded two new singles for RPM in January 1952 and later two more: 'You Didn't Want Me' and 'You Know I Love

You'. On September 13th of that same year, the latter song entered the charts and reached No. #1 in November, 1952. In his songs, B.B. usually took out any references to violence and sexuality although these were often common themes in pre-World War II blues. He was anxious not to alienate groups in the African-American community who didn't really like the content of his hit single 'You Upset Me Baby'. B.B. would later say,

> "Still sold over a million of 'em!" [20]

Very early B.B. autograph, inscribed with song title 'You Upset Me' (Collection of Richard Booth)

B.B. King's new string of hits, from 'Three O' Clock Blues' to 'Sweet Little Angel', would make him one of the most in-demand artists on the African-American music scene during the 1950's. However, despite his growing success, he would still find time to head back to Memphis between tours to his wife and his WDIA broadcasts. He remembered:

> "'Like weekends I would go. I would go like to Atlanta. In fact, I've even went to Washington. I would go to the West Coast. Went to Los Angeles once during that time. But I'd leave like on Friday night and get off for that next day. Then play a

> *Saturday night and then I worked back. So I didn't go far. But I was always going someplace like St. Louis. I'd go there very easy. St. Louis, Atlanta, Houston. But most of the time it was within a hundred, two hundred mile radius."* [21]

King's constant touring eventually began to create problems with work and for his marriage. Martha was very jealous of B.B.'s female fans. Some of her reactions were unjustified; others were justified. Martha would finally ask for a divorce in 1952. B.B. was deeply affected for a long time, feeling that his music career had destroyed his marriage. Then, his work at WDIA suddenly came to an end in 1953. It seemed ill-timed but, at the same time inevitable with the way his career was taking off. After this happened, B.B. made a deal with Bill Harvey, a saxophonist who was leading the house band at the Club Handy.

> *"Harvey and I thought we had a pretty good combination, so we decided that we would go to Buffalo Booking Agency."* [22]

With his RPM recordings now entering the hit parade and his career becoming even bigger than before, B.B. would become a major mainstay in the Chitlin' Circuit. These were the African-American clubs nicknamed after a soul food dish made from hogs' intestines. Unfortunately, some promoters at these clubs would keep all the nights takings so the artists ended up with nothing! B.B. said later:

> *"A lot of the promoters couldn't afford to pay you very much money and if they didn't have a pretty good crowd, sometimes you didn't get paid at all."* [23] However, he would also say, *"I only have about $180,000 owed up to me from my playing during my career."* [24]

After 'Three O Clock Blues' became a hit B.B. would also *'go up a step'*, appearing almost exclusively in the best small town clubs and the most important theatres in the cities. His talent was so exceptional that his popularity had grown continuously since his first nationwide hit. This was evident as a record audience of 10,000 was crammed into Houston's City Auditorium to hear him in May of 1954. Some promoters during that time would greatly underestimate the number of fans wanting to see B.B. King in concert. In August 1954, when he played the Savoy Ballroom in Hollywood, more than 3,000 fans

B.B. King and Bill Harvey & Orchestra (Texas Music Collection)

were turned away. At this same time, B.B.'s financial position was improving, along with his playing career. From 1954, he became one of the top ten earners in the R & B field. B.B. began playing to an average attendance of 325,000 people, grossing approximately $480,000.[25]

In 1956, the first day of January found B.B. starting a thirty-date per month tour in Florida and he kept up this pace the entire year. He made 342 appearances in 366 days.[26] Evelyn Johnson of the Buffalo Booking Agency estimated that this was an all-time record for any entertainer, during that time and he was presented with a gold ring by his booking agency. In the mid 1950's, B.B.'s minimum fee per concert went from five hundred to seven hundred dollars and soon went over the one thousand dollar mark. This allowed B.B. to increase the size of his band which by this time numbered a dozen musicians. Apart from the musicians in his band, B.B. King's organisation included a road manager and his assistant, a driver for the new tour bus 'Big Red' and a chauffeur for B.B., who drove separately with him in his Cadillac [27]. Among the high points for B.B. King at this time would be a tour with Louis Jordan, one of his idols when he was growing up.

In 1956 'Blues Boy Recording Company' owned by B.B. King was created. His new company was successful, but ceased in late 1957 or early 1958 because of internal politics. [28] Touring also began to take its toll on B.B. due to his endless schedule. The band's day usually started with a 10-13 hour drive in the bus, after which they would have to set up on stage. This was followed by a 3-5 hour concert. Then they would take everything down before setting off for the next town and another show. Added to these demands, segregation was still in force throughout America and it was very difficult to find places for B.B. and the band to stay in and to eat.

Being on the road was also a dangerous place to be. During his career, B.B. King survived 15 car and bus wrecks of which, the most serious left him with an open wound to his right arm and a number of severed ligaments. Yet, even after undergoing a major operation, B.B. still fulfilled his show that same evening. The most serious incident apart from that was a collision with a tanker, which ended 'Big Red's' life as the tour bus. The insurance company had just gone bust, so B.B. had to buy a new bus and pay out a huge amount of money to cover his liability. [29]

Through all these ups and downs, B.B. King still remained one of the most determined artists ever. During over a sixty year career, he cancelled less than twenty performances. During the majority of this career he performed an average of 330 times a year since he started out. This schedule had evened out at around 220 shows a year by 2002. It would drop later to a 'three days on and three days off' toward the end of his touring career which, sadly, ended many years later, suddenly, in October 2014.

B.B. would eventually remarry in June of 1958 and Sue Carol Hall became his second wife. He still continued to record hits which topped the charts. His releases always sold at least 50,000 copies including his best-selling LP, at that time, 'B.B. King Sings Spirituals'. Dedication, durability and an obsession with his music made B.B. King a better performer, as well as an inspiration and mentor to many. Several people who started out in the 1950's still remain deeply grateful to B.B. King for his advice and expertise, as well as for the moral and financial support he was always ready to give them. During 1956 Elvis Presley, who was just becoming famous at that time, expressed his heartfelt admiration and gratitude for what B.B. had taught him:

"Thanks man for the early lessons you gave me." [30]

(Photo: Jas Obrecht Music Archive)

THE BLUES IS DYING ...

"The blues is dying", B.B. King said during the mid-sixties. In the early 1960's, B.B.'s music began to decline in the charts due to Top 40 radio turning its back on his music. This was largely due to the Vietnam War, the 'swinging sixties' and the appearance of other new sounds. In 1966 B.B. King would also separate from his second wife. He said:

> "I think the main reason for us being separated was because of my travelling. Music is my life; blues is B.B. King. Yes, I've been a crusader for it ... Without the blues.... I couldn't live!" [31]

B.B. saw these changes happening and it was hard for him, but he was determined not to be forgotten.

> "It might have been rough, but I was surviving. I could still work 340 nights a year and I did. I wasn't walking behind the mule or driving a tractor. I was out there giving it my all." [32]

Then B.B. switched record labels from RPM to ABC Records. They were a bigger label, already having popular performers such as Ray Charles and Fats Domino-- and B.B. King would be the next! Sales were good, but not spectacular at first. B.B. was beginning to feel left out of the music limelight again when soul music began emerging as the new sound. He switched from the Buffalo Booking Agency to the Shaw Agency in New York and was shocked at the changes that began to occur. The 60's also saw a change in younger audiences' perception and respect toward a performer. For instance, one night at a show the MC introduced him:

> "Ladies and Gentleman, here's the blues singer, Mr. B.B. King ..."

The audience started booing him! He was totally *"shocked, hurt and confused"*[33] as he later remembered, but he picked up Lucille, changed his set and started with 'Sweet Sixteen'. Tears started rolling down his face as he was singing, but when he stopped, he heard cheers replace the earlier boos.

One of the only records that helped B.B. King during this change in American musical tastes would be Louis Jordan's 'How Blues Can You Get'. Critics had eventually begun once again rediscovering the blues and in 1966, B.B. managed to regain the highest position of record sales at that time. 'Don't Answer the Door' would reach No. #2 on the Billboard charts. Then, in 1967, after hit and miss releases with ABC, two of B.B.'s most outstanding albums were released: 'Blues Is King' and 'Live at the Regal'. Both albums were recorded live in Chicago.

It is also worth noting that even though the 60's saw a change in music tastes, B.B. still continued to tour non-stop. Not long after his second divorce, he had moved to New York. He wanted to put some distance between his failed marriage and problems; his booking agency and record company also worked out of New York. This led to a chance meeting with a man named Sidney A. Seidenberg that would soon become a significant event in B.B. King's career. He had already hired a succession of managers, some good and some bad, and B.B.'s most recent at that time was a man named Louis Zito. After a few years, in 1968, a financial dispute arose between them - B.B. thought Zito was ripping him off. They both called in the services of Sid Seidenberg, who was an accountant working in New York. After a few months looking at the situation, Seidenberg showed his impartiality by pointing out that, although Zito was right, there *were* some inadequacies in his management.

B.B. was impressed by Seidenberg's honesty and competence, so he tried to persuade Seidenberg to take charge of his own business. "*B.B. made me a manager*", said Seidenberg, and right from the start, Sid Seidenberg sought *"high"* things for B.B. King.[34] He involved B.B. in many advertising campaigns including one with Pepsi-Cola. He also booked him in new, different ways and with different agencies. In 1968, B.B. King would also be approached by Hollywood. He was to perform songs for a film by ABC film productions entitled 'For the Love of Ivy' starring Sidney Poitier. His recordings, 'You Put It On Me' and 'The B.B. Jones' also became good sellers that year. 'Paying The Cost To Be The Boss' became an additional huge hit as a result of this newfound exposure.

A new producer next began work with B.B. named Bill Szymczyk. Bill helped to create the idea of putting a live side and a studio side together on one album. The result was B.B. King's 'Live and Well'. The 'Live' side was recorded in New York, featuring songs such as 'Don't Answer the Door' and 'Sweet Little Angel'. The 'Well' side was made at the New York studio of 'Hit Factory'. Szymczyk's aim was to sell B.B. King to a younger audience by emphasising his electric guitar playing and providing a more rock oriented backing than had been used previously for blues recordings. Their biggest hit together was 'Why I Sing The Blues', a musical account of the 300 year exploitation of black people in America. This sad reality is reflected in the lyrics:

'When I first got the blues
They brought me over on a ship

*Man was standing over me and
A lot more with the whip
Everybody wanna know
Why I sing the blues
Well, I've been around a long time
I've really paid my dues'*

B.B.'s next album was also created to build on this new feel, but was seen by many to be disappointing. The final track, though, would become a huge, legendary music hit! 'The Thrill Is Gone' was borrowed from Roy Hawkins and was the first recording in which B.B. under the direction of Szymczyk used strings on the song. B.B. later recalled its importance:

> *"I liked it and when 'The Thrill Is Gone' was released, my cross over began."* [35]

'The Thrill is Gone' entered the Billboard bestseller lists on January 3, 1970. It's creation and success closed a decade that had been a difficult one for B.B. King and it eventually earned B.B. his first Grammy Award. After several years, he had finally managed to 'cross over' and win white America, thanks to his new manager Sid Seidenberg. In the summer of 1968, B.B. appeared at the famous 'Fillmore West Festival' to a mostly white audience. He remembered:

> *"The last time we had played there it was 95% black, in 1963. This time it was 95% white, I was shocked. Mike Bloomfield introduced me as the greatest blues man. I didn't know if I should walk out there. When I finally did, they gave me a standing ovation. I wanted to cry. Words can't say how I felt."* [36]

B.B. King's new devoted white audiences were people who would frequent hippie promoter Bill Graham's Fillmore West and later attended rock festivals like Woodstock. His beloved 'Lucille' was the focus for these kids since the rock music celebrated at Woodstock was symbolised by the electric guitar. This was a new culture endorsed by Jimi Hendrix and Pete Townshend. In just a few months, rock music and stars had enabled B.B. King to become much more widely known. B.B. later commented on this:

> *"Until the days of rock n roll, a lot of the places just wouldn't accept us. In some of these places, the doors open now for you to go into."* [37]

In 1968, B.B. would be invited to perform at the Newport Folk Festival. Then, in 1969, he would rock the Newport Jazz Festival and the Texas International Pop Festival. Many television appearances quickly followed, including numerous appearances on 'The Tonight Show'. By the end of the sixties, B.B. King had toured all over the United States and Europe. When he returned with his full band a year later to London, the crowd went crazy. B.B. loved his fans but their excitement was almost overwhelming:

> 'We came through customs and there were about 2,300 people waving American flags. And as we walked through customs, everybody started hollering, 'B.B.! B.B.!' By God, I was frightened ... I'd never seen anything like that before. Never ever! I was actually like a superstar to them, at least that's the way they treated me!" [38]

Another important episode in B.B. King's career, following the Fillmore West, was participating in a 1970 tour by the Rolling Stones. Mick Jagger and his band wanted to pay their respects to the blues by *"presenting the sources of their inspiration to their concert audiences."* [39] It now seemed that after years of anxiety for him, B.B. King and his blues music had truly arrived. The blues were now definitely alive and well! In ten years, B.B. King had won over a worldwide audience – and without cutting himself off from his origins. Once began, this trend continued to grow for him in the years that followed.

Early tour poster with The Rolling Stones

B.B. King Award
(Collection of B.B. King)

B.B. King Playboy Hall of Fame Award
(Collection of Richard Booth)

KING WORLDWIDE

1970 was a great year for B.B. King. He premiered in Las Vegas, Nevada at Caesar's Palace and appeared on the popular 'Ed Sullivan Show'. He also recorded 'The Thrill is Gone' (taken from the 1969 LP 'Completely Well'), as a stand-alone 45 single. This hit song had had an immediate impact on the music charts. B.B. also played at Chicago's Cook County Jail which was released on LP. 'Live at Cook County Jail' would represent an important episode in B.B. King's career. The set list for this album was created from a collection of slow blues with which B.B. and his audience established a long lasting connection. Guitar Player magazine would name B.B. King the 'World's Top Blues Guitarist' in early 1970:

"The world opened her arms' to B.B. King and his blues." [40]

In February 1971, B.B. toured Japan. He went there as an 'Ambassador of the Blues' as no blues singer had ever played in Japan before. Since then, he would play many more tours in Asia, Europe and Australia. He was even welcomed to perform in Africa several times. Another important trip B.B. made was to the Holy Land. When he played Israel, he later said, *'We were sold out in Jerusalem'*.[41] On November 23, 1973, B.B. would join Sly and the Family Stone for a televised concert. Then, in October 1974, he joined John Lee Hooker and violinist Papa John Creach on 'Midnight Special', a late night television variety show.

In 1970, after The Beatles mentioned B.B. King's name in 'Dig It', a song on their album 'Let It Be', it became fashionable for the New York society elite to turn up at B.B.'s concerts. When Jackie Onassis came to a show at Manhattan's 'Bottom Line' press reports were full of the news and Sid Seidenberg was over the moon with the publicity it gathered. Famous guest artists also began making their way onto B.B.'s

LPs. "B.B. King in London', released on October 11, 1971, featured Beatle Ringo Starr, Alexis Korner and Peter Green. B.B. now seemed to understand the truly universal appeal his music was having on listeners worldwide:

> *"When I sing a blues, the whole song may not be about the person, but there are certain things in it that they will recognise that have happened to them, or some of their friends and when this happens, they feel it."* [42]

By the mid-seventies, B.B. wanted to move away from the hustle and bustle of New York. Eventually he decided to settle in Las Vegas, the city he would call home for the remainder of his life. He rarely had more than a few days there at a time, though, due to his constant, non-stop touring commitments throughout the world. He would also take his blues to Ghana, Largos, Chad and Liberia. On one tour, B.B. performed in Zaire for the Muhammad Ali vs. George Foreman fight 'Rumble in the Jungle'. His appearance there can be seen on the 'B.B. King Live in Africa' video and DVD. Another major accolade for B.B. would be winning the blues category at the 11th Annual WHA CD image awards. In 1978, at the request of the State Department, B.B. performed in Mexico. He and his band were representing the USA at the International World Cultural Festival.

In 1979, B.B. also became one of the first American contemporary musicians to tour Russia in co-operation with the United States State Department and Soviet Union cultural exchange. He would also become a regular entertainer on the college circuit and at jazz and blues festivals throughout the world. Yet, even after becoming a world figure, Riley B. King never forgot his humble roots and the poverty and social inequities he had witnessed around him. After events like 'Live at Cook County Jail', he began devoting as much time as he could to playing free concerts for inmates in correctional institutions and prisons across the United States.

In 1973, B.B. received his first of a series of honorary college degrees. His first was a LHD from Tougaloo College in his home state of Mississippi. In 1977, Yale University presented B.B. with an Honorary Doctorate of Music. Later, the Berklee College of Music honoured him with a Doctorate of Music degree in 1982, and Rhodes College of Memphis also presented him with an Honorary Doctorate of Fine Arts in 1990. The only setback for B.B. during the 70's was a growing tension in his artist-management relationship, as Seidenberg was also representing Gladys Knight and the Pips and negotiating an important television contract for her. By July of 1975, B.B. began to feel as if he was being unfairly neglected and decided to leave Seidenberg's management and begin to manage his own affairs. Seidenberg remembered:

> *"The first thing I did when I took over in 1968 was to get rid of the bus. The first thing he did when he went out on his own in 1975 was to buy another bus. Right away it broke down, He had to get a new engine."* [43]

Early in 1978, B.B. and Sid were back together again. In his absence, B.B. didn't have the business contacts Sid had earlier used to enhance his growing career. Another factor in their reunion was that in 1977, Gladys Knight and the Pips split up which left Seidenberg without a star act. The main indicator thatced the B.B. King-Seidenberg team had returned was a surge of new B.B. King album recordings. Sid's new, priority management aim was to restore the great B.B. King dynamism that had somehow leveled out over the prior few years.

In late 1981, B.B. King made the album 'There Must Be a Better World Somewhere' for MCA, who had bought ABC in 1979. In the late 80's, B.B. also recorded songs and wrote the film score for the movie 'Into the Night'. From this John Landis film, which was a major media success, B.B. King's fame gained another considerable boost. B.B. also appeared in the movie, himself, and sang three numbers on the soundtrack. These were given airplay as video clips on MTV which gave way to a newer younger audience. In 1984 during a concert at the Beverly Theater in Los Angeles, Michael Jackson and Prince, who wanted to show their respect for the "King" and his music, joined B.B. onstage.

In 1986 B.B. also sang for the film 'The Colour of Money' and was again back in demand by film studios in 1987 for 'Stormy Monday'. He also had a small part in a film called 'Amazon Women on the Moon'. During the following years, he would also make a number of guest appearances on television programmes including, Baywatch, General Hospital and The Cosby Show. The National Academy of Recording Arts and Sciences would honour B.B. King with a Lifetime Achievement Award in 1987. In 1988, U2 also paid homage to B.B., when Bono wrote 'When Love Comes to Town' especially for him. B.B. had met the group backstage after a show and asked Bono to write a song for him. His musical gift to B.B. appeared on U2's successful 'Rattle and Hum' album. Thanks to airplay on MTV, that song, 'When Love Comes to Town' was seen and loved by millions of fans from all musical tastes and styles the world over. B.B. recognized the importance of this song:

> *"A lot of young people that listen and like rock n' roll, they've been introduced to myself through U2 including through video and television."* [44]

B.B. King visited the White House Oval Office in 1989 and he also performed a highly regarded concert at the Kennedy Center for the Performing Arts in January of 1990 to honour President George Bush on the first anniversary of his inauguration. The following years (1990-1991) also became a very busy time for B.B. King with three new CD's issued. These included his two live albums, 'Live at San Quentin' and then 'Live at the Apollo' with the Philip Morris Orchestra. B.B. would win a Grammy for 'Live at San Quentin'. In 1994, he performed a series of sold-out concerts in South America and embarked on a Far East tour. This took him to China, where he helped open the Hard Rock Café in Beijing.

In 1996, B.B. King would receive the respected 'Kennedy Center Honors' from President Bill Clinton. Another highlight for B.B. that year would be seeing his name at the top of the bill for the 'Southern Jamboree', which closed the Atlanta Olympic Games on August 4, 1996. His own autobiography, 'Blues All Around Me' was also released that year. It was another huge achievement, among so many more, for a very special person with a highly successful and distinguished career.

It was at about this time that I formed my own B.B. King Fan Club Website and began to eagerly anticipate finally meeting B.B. King myself.

B.B. King passes and badges
(Collection of Richard Booth)

Letter from B.B. King
(Collection of Richard Booth)

Early 'bluesboyking' fan club and web site flyers
(Collection of Richard Booth)

RETURNING HOME

In 1983 B.B. King returned to Indianola, Mississippi for a homecoming show. He came home to the place where he had once worked hard from 'sun to sun' for as little as 35 cents a day. He was 57 years old at the time, and it had almost been four decades since the day B.B. left the cotton plantation he once laboured on, in search of fame. It was a 'gala event'. The press came from all around the world to see the homecoming of the 'King of the Blues'. B.B. said on that special day in June 1983:

> *"For the first time in my life, I don't feel like I'm the prodigal son anymore. I feel like I'm home."* [45]

A party was given with 125 leading members of the white community and an equal number of black leaders in attendance. It was the first time these community leaders from both races had mingled together on a social basis. The two-lane street that fronted Gentry High School was renamed 'B.B. King Road' in his honour. A festival and concert was also staged. For B.B. King this was a very proud moment in time. He said:

> *"I've been back to Indianola a number of times. Last night, being able to shake hands with the elite of Indianola on a social basis, as well, that was my real homecoming."* [46]

In 1984, B.B. King was inducted into the Blues Hall of Fame. Then, in 1986, he was inducted into the Rock N' Roll Hall of Fame, in honour of his influence on rock artists like Eric Clapton and Mike Bloomfield. Performance Awards Polls also would vote B.B. King 'Blues Act of the Year' in 1985, 1987 and 1988. During the next decade B.B.'s recognition and acclaim grew further. On February 19, 1991, the first Orville H. Gibson Lifetime Achievement Award was presented to him at a ceremony at the Hard Rock Café in New York City. On February 20, he won his fifth Grammy Award, taking the 'Best Traditional

Blues Recording' category. Since 1969, B.B. King has received over eighteen Grammy Awards.

In late 1991, B.B. took advantage of modern video technology and performed on a three-part instructional video series. It was structured like a documentary and the videos featured B.B. King and his band in performance, as well as comments from B.B. on his major musical influences and experiences over King's 40 year career. This series was later re-released on DVD format through Warner Brothers and DCI Music. Most would admit, even with instruction, it would be a challenge to "learn" B.B. King. He had a unique style that cannot be duplicated:

> *"When I sing, I play in my mind, the minute I stop singing orally, I start to sing by playing Lucille..."* [47]

He also had a special way of closing his eyes while he interpreted the blues lyrics that made him famous.

> *"You can see why my wife Martha used to call me ol' lemon face."* [48]

B.B. once explained how he felt during his playing:

> *"When I'm singing, I see the person in my mind whom I'm singing about. If something clouds my memory while I'm singing, let's say somebody in the band laughs, I can still sing. But it's not real anymore. The spell is broken."* [49]

B.B. King would continue his non-stop touring regime until October of 2014, entertaining millions of fans all over the world. There was never a time to ask B.B. if he was ready to retire. He said at one of his shows in Manchester, England:

> *"People say of me retiring. How can I retire with music like this!"* [50]

B.B. also commented about the possibility of him retiring a few years ago:

> *"I don't have to work as hard as I do. But I couldn't have stopped before, even for a short while, as some of my ladies pleaded for me to do. If I had, the blues would no longer be alive. I hope my kids will forgive me. I hope they understand why I was never there."* [51]

During his life, B.B. King did manage to receive what he had always wanted - 'worldwide acceptance':

> *"The idea that my blues have been accepted gives me peace of mind. I don't say this to boast, but the truth is that I've become a millionaire. I'm proud of that fact because, as you know by now, it wasn't easy. Solid investments, thanks to Sid, have given me security in my old age."* [52]

B.B. King's real life is a fantastic tale of his difficult early upbringing, working on the Delta plantation, and of all his hard work trying to break into the music business. He did finally achieve worldwide status as the King of the Blues and he deserved it whole-heartedly. His status today also confirms his place as the finest blues artist of our generation.

His lifetime achievements were unending. He opened B.B. King Blues Clubs in Memphis, Los Angeles, Las Vegas and New York and helped open the Foxwoods Casino. Gibson guitars produced a line of B.B. King 'Lucille' models, including the Gibson and Epiphone guitars, and B.B. King guitar strings. A casual clothing line was created, food products, barbecue sauce, salad dressing, salsa and bean spreads. There was even talk about B.B. King frozen catfish! During his life, B.B. also enjoyed doing several commercials over the years. These included one for M&Ms and a Budweiser commercial using his music. He also became a spokesman for television ads targeted toward controlling and treating diabetes. His biggest compliment of all came from North West Airlines. They not only put him on their TV advertisements but, for his 70th birthday, they also painted 'Lucille' and wrote 'Happy Birthday B.B. King' on one of their jets. B.B. King also received numerous trophies and plaques during this lifetime. He once said:

"I've gotten enough trophies and plaques to fill a garage!" [53]

B.B. King was invited to the White House by every President from George Bush to Barack Obama. Queen Elizabeth and Prince Philip also invited B.B. to a garden party they were hosting while in Washington D.C. Mr. King said that he felt uncomfortable because the place was full of famous people. Lots of people were approaching B.B. to speak to him. The Reverend Jesse Jackson noticed this and remarked:

"Looks like more people are lining up to see the 'King' than the Queen!"

When B.B. was not touring (which did not add up to many free days!), he loved to enjoy his extensive collection of records, books and videotapes. He also had a love for his cars. These included a Mercedes and a Rolls Royce, but it was his GMC low rider truck that he loved to attend to and take out over the Nevada desert. That was where he could, as B.B. himself put it: *"Forget my troubles."* [54]

B.B. also loved computers and always took his two laptops on tour in order to keep up to date with the latest technology, email and Internet. He used one of his laptops for games, (*"Solitaire's got me hooked"*, he once said). The other laptop he used for general information, courses on music theory and even for a course on mathematics. As he once said:

"Anything to keep my aging mind from getting rusty." [55]

He also would produce a CD-Rom version of his life story in 1996 and open up his website: 'www.bbking.com'. His website kept fans all over the world up to date on the latest news about him, tour dates, photos and other information. B.B. King always looked after his health, too, as he had diabetes. He had even given up smoking early in his career and drinking later. The only can you would ever see B.B. drinking in his dressing room after a show was a can of Diet Coke. He would pretend it was a beer! His band was always fantastic and B.B. loved playing shows with them - night after night. Most of the band members had been performing with him for several years. B.B. also loved to be around younger musicians because he believed we could learn so much from them.

When once asked to sum up his life, B.B. King recognised modestly that there would be more and greater achievements ahead of him in the years that followed. He was able to unaffectedly accept that he had become a success:

> "I've been asked that before, if there was anything I would do differently if I had this life to start again. And there are only two things I can think of that I would change. I would finish high school and go to college and try to learn more about the music and I wouldn't marry until after forty" [56]

(Photo: André Hobus Photo Library)

B.B. and the author in Manchester during the 1999 UK tour.

B.B. King Worldwide: Passes and Tickets (Collection of Richard Booth)

B.B. and me in his dressing room, backstage at the Bridgewater Hall, Manchester, England, July 3, 2001.

MEETING B.B. KING

B.B. King really cared about his fans. Night after night he gave out guitar pins and picks to fans after each show. He signed hundreds of autographs and posed for photos with everyone who wanted one. Nobody was ever left out and he never refused anyone. B.B. once said:

> *"As a guitar player, I look for harmony among notes. As a human being, I look for harmony among people."* 57

I was one of those many fans who loved his music and respected the man that was B.B. King. He was one of those rare commodities who loved what he did and never lost sight of the people who put him there, always showing him their love and affection. This love was reciprocated by B.B. in a two-way process that lasted throughout his whole career.

I wanted to share my love and passion for this great man and provide a mechanism for sharing all the wonderful concerts I attended. As a kid I had been a member of the Kiss and Elvis Presley fan clubs and loved to receive newsletters and information about the artist and their music and not miss out on anything! When I heard B.B.'s music and became his devoted fan, I also wanted to act as a channel for all the news, reviews, and photos that were constantly being distributed about him throughout the world.

This was the reason behind my creation of what was first a B.B. King Fan Club and much later a United Kingdom B.B. King website: to provide a way for his fans to gain all the latest information, bring people together as a community and to share our love of B.B. and his music. I knew it would be hard work. I had previously produced and managed fanzines for a number of bands since the late 80's and wanted the B.B. fan club and website to be extra special. The advent of bluesboyking.com in 1999 made the process easier for me to reach thousands of people - even more people than the actual printed fanzines could. It became all the more special for me that B.B. knew about my fan club's existence and would always take an interest in its development whenever we spent time together. I have loved producing my site and bringing news and exclusive photos of the shows where I have been fortunate enough to see B.B. up close at over the years.

Meeting B.B. King in person was an unforgettable experience. I have had the privilege of meeting him many times at various hotels when he has been in town for concerts. I have also met him, on his own ground, backstage in his dressing room after shows. It was there that he would take time to meet fans who had waited patiently to see him. He also signed many autographs and fulfilled most requests. Although B.B. King was the ultimate performer, also awarded 'Entertainer of the Year' at the 2002 W.C. Handy Blues Awards in Memphis, he still remained throughout his life, the friendliest person you could ever wish to meet. I always looked forward to and cherished the moments when we could chat together and discuss all manner of things. B.B. was a very articulate and friendly person and even though time was limited, he always spoke to me (sometimes for hours!). I would soon begin to affectionately refer to him as "B". This was the endearment that many of those close to him used.

He was always excited about what he was doing musically. It was that passion and dedication on his behalf that was infectious and led me to adopt the same dedication for his fans across the world. Year after year, he loved music more than ever and it showed every time I saw him play a show. He said he was always:

> "...still thrilled to pick up Lucille in the privacy of my hotel room or at a public concert and have her soothe my troubled mind. Still looking for the right blues notes and right blues sounds that paint private feelings words can't describe." [58]

When he was alive, B.B. thought a lot about his future and mentioned that he would like:

> "...the excitement to keep coming till I die. I don't fear death. When I think of death, I have three preferences. That I will die in my sleep or holding Lucille while playing on stage or holding a woman while making love." [59]

When someone asked B.B. King about the state of the blues in the millennium, he was said to comment:

> "I'd say the blues are prospering." [60]

After many years of being a huge fan of B.B.'s and the music that is B.B. King, as well as running the UK fan club, I still continue to include news, reviews, photos, biography, discography, anything and everything to do with the King of the Blues. My website has become very popular with fans of B.B. all over the world. I update the site frequently and at one time I did this as often as three or four times a day! It was also for my fan club and website followers that I reviewed and photographed B.B. at many of his shows across the UK. Many of these one of a kind photos are included in this book. Even with B.B.'s tragic passing, fans can still visit my website to exchange messages about shows they have been to, their memories or just to acknowledge their appreciation of B.B. King on my message board.

I had been very fortunate to have had front row seats for 'B's last few tour appearances before his passing. It was a great feeling to witness B.B. King so close, seeing him doing what he loved best - playing his blues. I was also lucky enough to be invited by B.B. to chat for nearly an hour at his hotel in 2001. He had just flown from Milan, Italy to Manchester, England. He had missed a flight, had a long wait at the airport and was really tired, but B.B. still made enough time to invite me to sit and chat about the current tour, blues singers, guitars (of which he signed my Gibson that afternoon), computers and life in general. He asked me if I taught the guitar, *"as I could give him a few lessons"*. I sensed he was joking but I responded in earnest, *"You don't need any lessons 'B'!"* His reply to me was some advice, which I feel manifested the great B.B. King's philosophy on life:

> *"You are always learning, Richard. Whatever you do, don't ever forget that."* [61]

Tickets for the 2006 UK tour (Collection of Richard Booth)

B.B. King would visit the UK in 2006 to perform his farewell tour. He was 80 years old at the time and had decided to wind down his exhaustive schedule. B.B.'s struggle with diabetes had still not changed his non-stop touring commitments, as he continued to entertain millions of fans throughout the world.

B.B. King Tour Laminate (Collection of Richard Booth)

B.B. King tour flyer for the Farewell Tour: March/April 2006

The author and B.B. backstage during the 2006 UK tour.

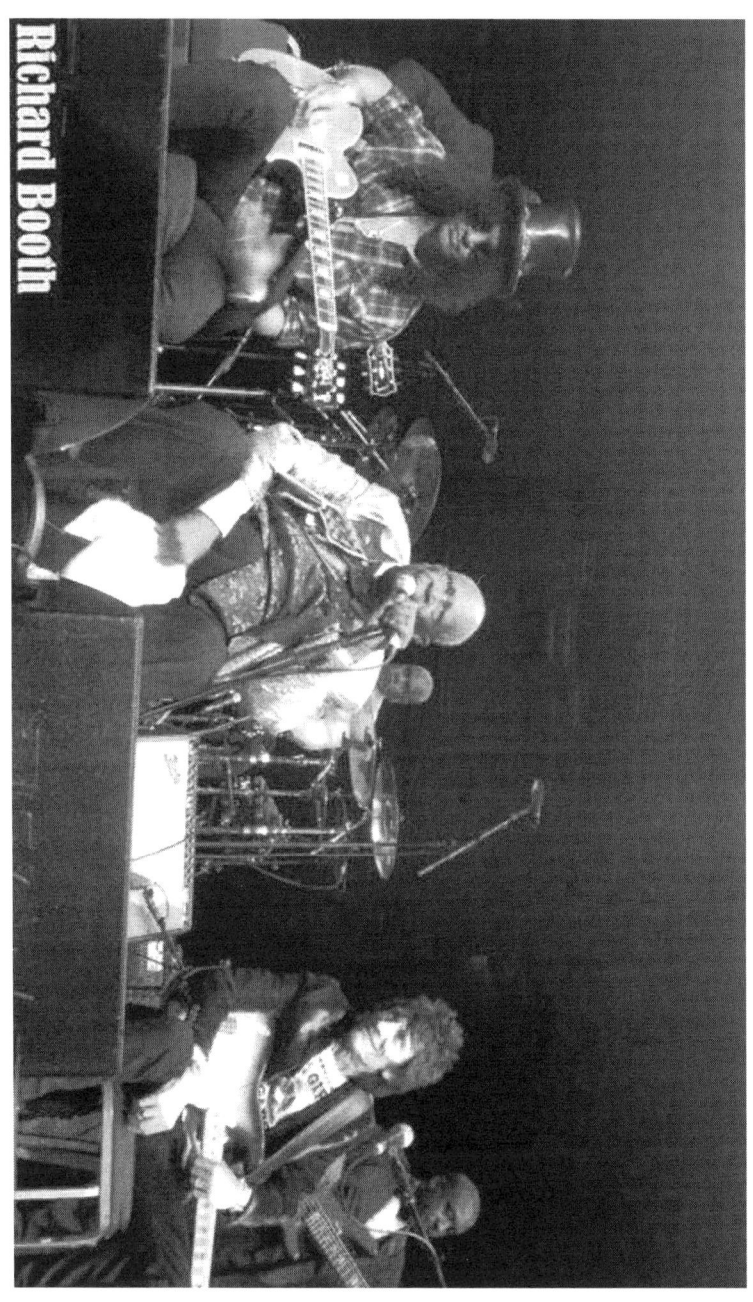

Slash, B.B. and Ronnie Wood at Royal Albert Hall, London 2011 (Photo: Richard Booth)

Royal Albert Hall show flyer, June 28, 2011

B.B. and the author at the Royal Albert Hall June 2011 (Collection of Richard Booth)

LATER YEARS

Although the 2006 World Tour was billed as a 'farewell', B.B. King remained very active afterward during the final years of his life. The 2006 tour featured special guest guitarist Gary Moore, with whom B.B. had previously toured and recorded, and included the song 'Since I Met You Baby'. The tour began in the United Kingdom, and continued worldwide with highlight performances at the Montreux Jazz Festival and the Blues at Sunset event in Zürich. During B.B.'s show in Montreux at Stravinski Hall, he jammed with Joe Sample, Randy Crawford, David Sanborn, Gladys Knight, Stanley Clarke, John McLaughlin and Barbara Hendricks.

B.B. had always looked forward to playing with other celebrated artists and friends during many of his shows. He fed off the musical talents of others and you could always see the happiness and awe in his face on stage. That response was a true joy to witness every time it happened. The musicians in the B.B. King Blues Band also always brought out this emotion in his face. He was overjoyed to be amongst them on stage every night--and they watched his *every* move for pinpoint precision timing. They were the backbone of the band, but B.B. was the band leader-- and he was right on the money every time!

In June 2006, King would be present when he was honoured at a commemoration of his first radio broadcast at the Three Deuces Building in Greenwood, Mississippi where an official marker of the Mississippi Blues Trail was erected. That same month, a ground breaking was held in Indianola, Mississippi for a new museum dedicated to the life and career of Riley B. King. The B.B. King Museum and Delta Interpretive Center opened on September 13, 2008. It was to the grounds of that museum that B.B. King would later journey to reach his final resting place.

In late October 2006, B.B. King began recording a concert album, also filmed for DVD release entitled 'B.B. King: Live'. It was filmed over four nights at his B.B. King Blues Clubs both in

B.B. King Concert tickets (Collection of Richard Booth)

Nashville and Memphis, Tennessee. Released in 2008, it was B.B.'s first live performance recording in over a decade. It captured his show as he performed it nightly around the world. He also played at Eric Clapton's second Crossroads Guitar Festival in 2007 and contributed the song 'Goin' Home' to the collection 'Goin' Home: A Tribute to Fats Domino'. B.B. also sang "One Shoe Blues" on Sandra Boynton's children's album: 'Blue Moo' and was accompanied by a pair of sock puppets in a music video for the song. His musical contributions and appearances were always heartfelt and well received.

In the summer of 2008, two big events in B.B.'s career also took place. He performed at the Bonnaroo Music and Arts Festival in Manchester, Tennessee, where he was given a 'Key to the City'. He was also inducted into the Hollywood Bowl Hall of Fame, an accolade that meant a lot to B.B. He had played many shows at that famous venue and this award was a fitting tribute to B.B.: the 'King of the Blues'. Then, in 2009, B.B. was back again in Europe and the UK to perform a few select shows (including Wembley Arena in London) before flying back to the United States to continue his constant touring schedule.

The following year, King would travel back across the world to perform at the Mawazine Festival in Rabat, Morocco on May 27, 2010, and in June of that same year, B.B. performed again at the Crossroads Guitar Festival with Robert Cray, Jimmie Vaughan, and Eric Clapton. He also contributed to Cyndi Lauper's album 'Memphis Blues', which was released on June 22, 2010. Then, in 2011, B.B. once again graced the UK and Europe with his presence. He played at the legendary Glastonbury Music Festival, receiving a rapturous reception in front of the 90,000+ crowd. His amazing performance later at the Royal Albert Hall in London on June 28, 2011 was recorded live and produced by Jon Brewer for the CD/DVD and Blu-ray release.

Jon Brewer also directed the excellent full-length, in-depth documentary on B.B. titled 'The Life of Riley', which was released in 2012. Jon worked closely with B.B. for over two years to create this fantastic visual film. It covered the life and times of B.B. King with great contributions from a number of people who knew B.B. the best throughout his life, including his ex-wife Sue Hall, musicians Buddy Guy, Eric Clapton, Bono and many more. This outstanding film provides the only documentary ever produced on B.B. King's celebrated life and contains some rare archival footage and interviews

On February 21, 2012, B.B. was among the legendary performers who appeared 'In Performance at the White House: Red, White and Blues', during which President Obama sang part of 'Sweet Home Chicago' with B.B. and Buddy Guy. That same year B.B. would also record songs for the debut album of rapper and producer Big K.R.I.T., who also hails from B.B.'s birthplace in Mississippi. On July 5, 2012 B.B. and his Blues Band performed a concert at the Byblos International Festival in Lebanon, delivering another well-received performance at this unique musical event. On May 26, 2013, he would also appear at the New Orleans Jazz Festival, which featured a headline set by Elton John.

A very rare occurrence would happen in November 2013 when B.B. King cancelled an Oklahoma City concert due to unsafe conditions on the roads leading into the city. During the months that followed, although B.B. continued his energetic schedule and devotion to his fans, his performances began less predictable. For instance, in St. Louis, Missouri in April of 2014, 'EW's The Music Mix' reported on a show B.B. King had given that evening. They sadly commented that B.B., the long-reigning master of blues music, had given a shaky performance. The concert was so erratic that B.B.'s spokesperson would issue a statement of apology following the gig. He lamented,

> *"The combination of the rigors of the very long drive and high blood sugar due to his medication error resulted in a performance that did not match Mr King's usual standard of excellence."* [62]

This occurrence was due to Mr. King's ongoing problems with Type II diabetes compounded by the 500 mile plus journey he had travelled for the show. Guitarist Hamish Anderson, whose band was appearing as the opening act during the trek, tweeted:

> ..."*Very sad to hear the news of B.B. King's sickness and subsequent cancellation of the tour. The band and I wish him a safe speedy recovery!*" [63]

Following this occurrence, during 2014, B.B. began to suffer from a further series of medical problems attributed to his long battle with diabetes. These gave way for great concern from his friends and family. On October 3, 2014, not feeling well enough to continue his tour, B.B. suddenly had to stop his live performance at the House of Blues in Chicago, Illinois. A doctor diagnosed him with dehydration and exhaustion and the eight remaining shows at B.B. King's Blues Club and Grill in New York had to be cancelled. King did not schedule any additional shows for the remainder of the year.

In October 8, 2014, B.B. King announced he was back at home to recuperate. Appreciation was expressed by B.B. for the concern and support he had received from his fans. Then, on May 1, 2015, after being hospitalized in Las Vegas on two occasions as a result of complications from high blood pressure and diabetes, King announced on his website (bbking.com), that he was in hospice care at his home in Las Vegas, Nevada. Sadly he was never able to recover from that series of incapacitating medical events and illness. Riley B. King passed away in his sleep on May 14, 2015 at the age of 89. The official cause of his death was determined to be multi-infarct dementia, brought on by a series of small strokes caused by Type II Diabetes. The Clark County coroner's office confirmed on May 25, 2015, that it would perform an autopsy. This later revealed that B.B.'s death was due to complications of Alzheimer's disease and congestive heart failure.

'One Kind Favor' album cover

TWO WHITE HORSES ...
and a GOLDEN CHAIN ...

All over the world, people would join together in deep mourning. I vividly remember the morning I received the call informing me of B.B.'s passing. I was in total shock. I just stood there and broke down, comforted by my wife. She knew what 'B' meant to me and was upset too. On my way to write the news, my daughters knew I was upset and cuddled up to me as I wrote the words for my website. They just said *"Sorry Dad, B.B. King, he was your friend."* I struggled with tears as I had to inform all of the fans in my fan club on the UK site and to break the news to the millions of fans throughout the world on social media. Every news channel and media site also ran stories, videos and photos to announce 'The King's' passing and to celebrate the wonderful life B.B. had lived and shared with the world.

(Photo: Courtesy of James Wessels)

On May 27, 2015, B.B. King was flown to Memphis for a series of tributes, memorials and public viewings. A big memorial concert took place in Beale Park featuring tributes by B.B.'s long-time band member and drummer Tony Coleman, Keb Mo, and Bobby Rush. His funeral procession was led down Beale Street, a brass band marching in front of the hearse, playing 'When the Saints Go Marching In' as thousands of mourners called out 'B.B.'! Rodd Bland, son of the late blues singer Bobby "Blue" Bland, carried the latest version of King's famous guitar 'Lucille'. Thousands lined the streets to pay their last respects.

(Photo: Courtesy of James Wessels)

B.B. King's body was then driven down Route 61 to his hometown of Indianola, Mississippi. He had made the long journey back to his home. After 60 years of travelling the world, and at his own request, B.B. King had come home to his final resting place. His body had been returned to his native Mississippi. About 500 people attended the services held at Bell Grove Missionary Baptist Church in Indianola. A further 200 people who couldn't get into the main room at the Church watched a live broadcast of the funeral in the Church's fellowship hall.

At the beginning of the service, family members filed past B.B.'s open casket, which had an image of Lucille embroidered on the padded white cloth inside the lid. Then, as the service began, the casket was closed and covered with a large arrangement of red roses. For nearly three hours, choirs sang songs of praise, while friends shared stories about the man who grew up dirt-poor in the Mississippi Delta, only to go on and change the world. Reverend Herron Wilson, who delivered the eulogy, spoke about Riley B. King's amazing life:

> *"How someone from such lowly and humble beginnings can rise to such noble heights of success?"* asked Williams. *"In many ways we can look at the life of B.B. King and be inspired and be encouraged. Hands that once picked cotton would someday pick guitar strings on a national and international stage. Amazing."* [64]

Stevie Wonder had also recorded an audio message that was played at the memorial service telling mourners,

"He will forever be the King of the Blues." [65]

(Photo: AAP)

Mississippi Governor Phil Bryant reminded mourners that B.B. was proud of being from Mississippi. While commenting on the thousands of people who had come to Indianola to show their respects, both at the public viewing on Friday and at the funeral on Saturday, Bryant said:

> *"He would have loved to know that one more time he's helping the Mississippi Delta."* Then, Bryant went on to say: *"We're going to continue to try to honor him every way we can from the state of Mississippi, to the Governor's Office, to the Senate, to the House, to the United States Congressmen, to U.S. Senators and Presidents. This humble, quiet man changed the world but the world never changed him."* [66]

Tony Coleman, B.B.'s drummer for 37 years, recalled that B.B. never referred to himself as 'King of the Blues', the honorary title others around the world used for him. Coleman said as he entered the church:

> *"He felt like the blues was the King, and it was his responsibility to keep it King,"* [67]

President Barack Obama and former President Bill Clinton each sent a letter giving tribute to B.B. King. These letters were read aloud by Democratic U.S. Rep. Bennie Thompson of Mississippi, a friend of King. Obama lamented, *"The blues has lost its king and America has lost a legend. No one worked harder than B.B. No one did more to spread the gospel of the blues."* President Clinton even recalled playing two gigs with King: *"I was his backup sax man",* [68] he said.

Riley B. King was buried and put to eternal rest at the B.B. King Museum and Delta Interpretive Center, the site he had visited years earlier. The museum has now developed a memorial garden, with benches and a water wall, around his grave. Allan Hammons, a board member of the Museum, had been with B.B. at a funeral a few years earlier. He mentioned that B.B. had told him on that day:

> *"I want you to pay special attention to the lyrics of the lead song on my new album."* [69]

'One Kind Favor' was King's last studio album and 'See That My Grave Is Kept Clean' (a cover of Blind Lemon Jefferson's hit) was the song B.B. had referred to. To Allan, later reflecting upon B.B.'s words, along with the meaning of the song, B.B. King had actually provided him with instructions for his own funeral. In the song, the lyrics state that 'he' wanted *"two white horses in a line and a grave dug with a silver spade"* and *"Let me down with a golden chain,"* he sang on the song. Allan Hammons intended to honour these final requests as best as he could. [70]

On Saturday, May 28, 2015, outside of the B.B. King museum, workers from Wilbert Funeral Services laid down straw to cover the mud by the empty gravesite. Wanda Clark, the project coordinator for the Mississippi Blues Trail, had the task of finding 'two white horses in a line'. *"White horses just aren't common around here,"* [71] she said, but through friends of friends, she had rounded them up. The horses arrived just after 2 p.m. One was a little stallion named 'Silver', and the other a Tennessee 'Walking Horse' named 'Rose'. In a third trailer was a beautiful black carriage horse that would carry a saddle draped with two of B.B. King's Lucille guitars.

The main honour guard led the way in the procession, followed by the 'two white horses in a line', then quickly followed by the black horse carrying the guitars. The weather turned bleak but the procession continued as the pallbearers got out of their vehicle and carried Riley B. King's casket to the grave. The minister for the service began, *"Earth to Earth. Ashes to Ashes. Dust to Dust."* [72] The general manager of Wilbert Funeral Services, Darwin May, had never heard of casket straps in a colour besides green.[73] Yet, he had received a request that somebody wanted another colour. To honour this request, a worker found a way to dye the straps and that afternoon there they were - holding up Riley B. King's coffin - *golden* in colour and chain-like in appearance, slowly letting B.B. King down into the ground.

(Photo: Hal Hannaford)

Memorial card given out at the public viewing, Memphis, May 2015 (Collection of Richard Booth)

Program given out at the funeral service, May 2015 (Collection of Richard Booth)

Tributes to Riley B. King
(Collection of Richard Booth)

THE THRILL IS GONE
BUT NEVER FORGOTTEN

B.B. had been unwell for a while, but nothing could prepare me or indeed millions of other people for the sad news that on May 14, 2015, Riley B King, the King of the Blues, affectionately known to fans as 'B.B. King', had passed away. Within a few days, musical tributes, memorial services and public viewings of B.B. were arranged. The news hit every major news, radio and television stations. Magazines ran tributes and dedicated memorial issues to celebrate the life and music of the great man. I created and have managed the B.B. King UK fan club and fan site www.bluesboyking.com for over 27 years. In that time I have had the pleasure to meet B.B. many times and to attend many shows here in the UK and Europe. It is still an honour and pleasure for me to run the site and interact with B.B. King fans worldwide.

I am very honoured that Mr. King himself continually viewed the site and followed its progress over the years. He always asked me how it was developing every time we met!

I have many special stories and have had several meetings

with Mr. King over the years. We chatted many times about his own musical heroes, music, guitars and life! I last met B.B. during his last UK tour in 2011, when he performed at a few shows; including Glastonbury and the Royal Albert Hall, (the latter which was filmed for the DVD and Blu-Ray release). At that show I had some items signed for the fan club to use as competition prizes and I also had an original sepia photo from the 1950's. B.B. had never seen that photo, so I gave that photo as a gift to Mr King. I could not think of anyone I would want to own that photo other than B.B. himself! He was so thrilled to receive it and that meant the world to me!

B.B. and his amazing music have been a huge part of my life and this has allowed me to witness some of the greatest shows and meet my hero on many, many occasions. I was honoured to call B.B. my friend and very proud to run his UK fan site and club. He was always a true gentleman and an Ambassador for the Blues - and indeed for every aspiring guitarist or any person. I feel very privileged that I had the opportunity to be involved with B.B. King. I always looked forward to seeing him. It is very difficult to realize that his concert appearances and our visits are no longer possible.

His legacy and memory will live on through his music and will continue to be enjoyed by millions of people worldwide and for future generations who have yet to hear his amazing catalogue of work. I will miss you my friend...

Richard Booth
July 2015

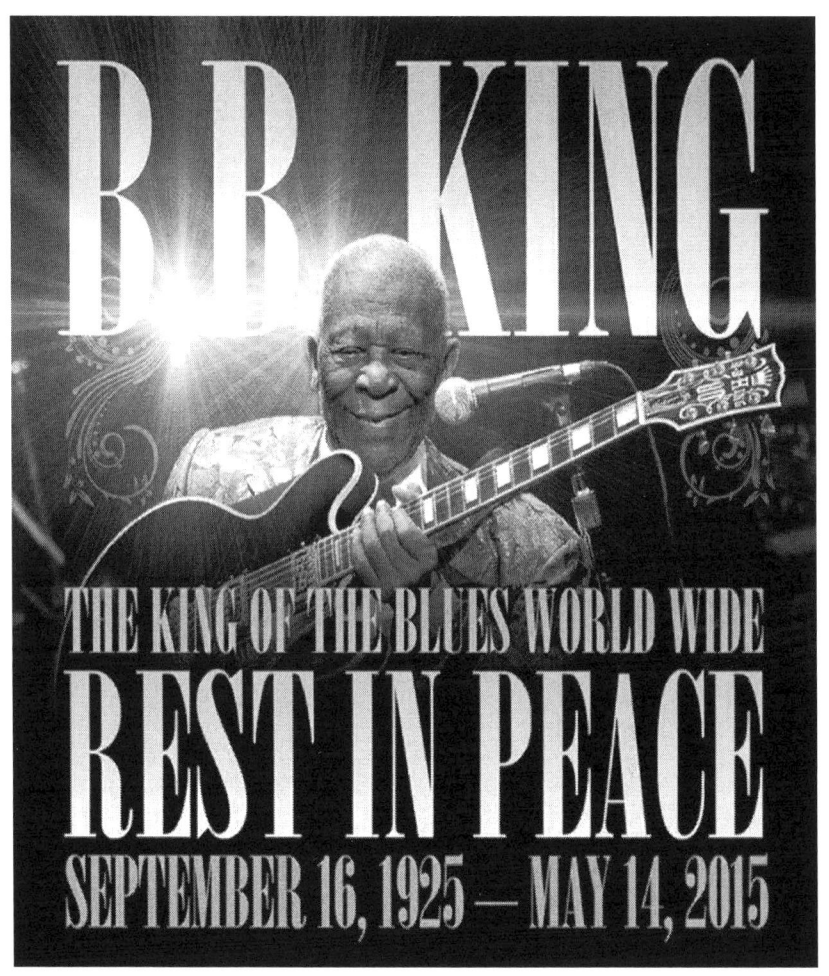

Tribute Poster, May 2015

Tribute to B.B. King Event flyer
Memphis, May 27, 2015

TRIBUTES

TO B.B. WITH LOVE

Tony Coleman

On September 16, 1978, I was performing on an International Blues tour and this was the first time I played with B.B King. He had his latest hit out 'Never Make a Move Too Soon' and I had the opportunity to play with B.B. I just began to play along and B.B's eyes opened wide and he said "Alright! You playing my new hit!" Later, someone said "You guys sound great, how would you guys like to play with B.B King?" We said "Hell Yeah!" I was 23 or something and was now playing with B.B King!

B.B offered me the job and that was it. It was September 16, 1978, B.B's birthday and he gave me his business card and said "Call my office on Sunday and we'll figure it all out". So every Sunday, I called the office and he said "Call me next Sunday, Call me next Sunday". So it was then January and he said "Ok, I'm ready to hire you now!" That's how we started playing with B.B. King.

B.B King, out of all the musicians, out of all the black American blues musicians, B.B was the cream of the crop. Other Blues bands looked like boy scouts, when you saw B.B and his band, they were always pristine. They looked very, very professional. B.B was always concerned with image. When we are on the road, you can't have an off day or have aches and pains. You just focus on doing the best shows possible and after we do the show, we can go off and be sick!

That's the way it was. I mean, you would drive from Atlanta, Georgia to Chicago and when you arrive to Chicago you have got to play a show and wouldn't have any rest. You get dressed and get on stage and kick ass and then you get some rest. Sometimes it was very difficult to do, but that is what B.B expected. He didn't expect any whining or cry-babies. All the time he was being professional.

What I learned from B.B was the humility he gave to fans and people. B.B would sit at the gate at the airport with all the other people, not in a separate room. Just with the regular passenger. Somebody would walk up to him and before you knew it there would be 5, 10, 20, 30 people around him and he would be nice to everybody. He would engage and talk to them. There was this humility in him. Afterwards, I would say to him, "Hey Boss" and he would say "Yes Tony Cole–Man?" He would always pronounce my last name like it was two names! I would say "Don't you get tired of people coming up to you all the time?" B.B would say "Well son, if I got tired I'd stay at home!"

He said "If it wasn't for all those people we would not be out here making a living and playing all these shows". I remember the humility part of him the most. I will miss that. A lot of people don't want to take time for fans. He would always take time and appreciated them as much as they appreciated him. My father was 'King Cole'. He created the dance: 'The Mash Potato' with James Brown. He was a famous disc jockey and produced a lot of acts at the Apollo Theater in New York, like Otis Redding and Rufus Thomas. My dad was friends with B.B. and Bobby 'Blue' Bland. They were good friends. When he hired me, he didn't know I was my father's son. When he found out he said "I got Coleman, I got him". My father said "Take care of him" and B.B. tried to keep me together. He was like a father figure. B.B was always trying to teach me, but I rejected a lot of things he was saying, because I thought he was 'old time'. But he would say to me "I know you don't like me telling you what to do son, but if you listen to me, one of these days when I'm dead and gone, you will remember everything I said and it will make sense to you later - and it does!

I can feel his presence and his spirit around me every day of my life. He was a mentor, a friend, not just as a blues player and musician I played with. He was like a father, an advisor and was a lot bigger than just a blues musician. I would put him in the category of Gandhi or Martin Luther King, that's the way I look at him and I appreciate him more now than I ever have and it makes sense to me. He came up in the era that he came up in.

He wanted me to be who I was, but he wanted me to also be able to understand where he was coming from.

As long as I am alive, through my music and my attitude, I will always be the way B.B was and how he treated people. That is how I will continue a legacy of excellence and humanity to the world. When people say "Blues", the first person you think of is B.B King and love, because B.B King is the Blues. Bono wrote a good song for B.B 'When Love Comes to Town'. That is what B.B was about and everybody did have love for him and he did for them. He was a part of my life and my growth.

Tony Coleman

Tony Coleman
August 10, 2015

John Mayall

"I first became aware of B.B. King in 1956 when a friend of mine played me a 78 rpm record of his and from the moment I heard that voice I was hooked and inspired for life. Back then in London I couldn't have imagined I'd be, not only meeting him, but playing regularly on the same stage in concerts with him throughout the world.

He was a major influence on my singing and someone who will be long remembered as truly a great friend and mentor."

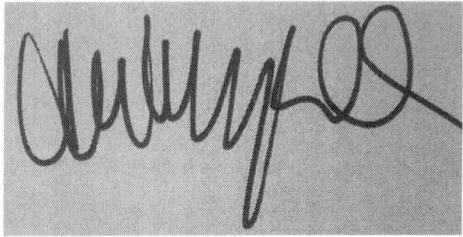

John Mayall
August 11, 2015

John Mayall and B.B.

John Mayall tribute to B.B. King, May 2015

B.B. King & John Mayall UK Tour flyer
June 2009

Walter Trout

When I was a teenager, I was working in a shopping mall, in a department store and this was in southern New Jersey. I was the guy who stocked the shelves and I worked there after school and on weekends. A buddy of mine came running into the store and he said "B.B. King's in the record shop!" There was a record shop in the shopping mall. He goes "B.B. King is in there looking at blues records". So I just walked out of my job. I figured I might get fired for this, but how often do you get this kind of opportunity? I walked over there and I had a piece of paper and I went up and said "Mr King, I am one of your biggest fans and could I get an autograph?" He started asking me about me and I said "Well, I really want to be a blues guitar player, that's what I want to do. I practice all the time, practice after school and I listen to all the records and I'm really trying hard". And he ended up standing in that record store with me and he talked to me for over an hour. It was incredible.

He seemed genuinely interested in talking to me. I'll never forget, he finally signed the autograph and he wrote "To Walter, keep playing, B.B. King". Unfortunately, the autograph got lost over the years as I went through homelessness, divorces and addictions. But that conversation... he was just the nicest, most genuine man. Years later when I was with John Mayall, we started doing a lot of shows with B.B. and the first show we did was at the Universal Amphitheatre in Los Angeles. I went in and started talking to him and said "Well, I'm playing guitar with John Mayall." He was really interested and happy to meet me and incredibly charismatic and I happened to mention to him "Well, I met you when I was sixteen in a record store!" He said "Well, I'm sorry, but I don't remember." I didn't expect him to remember but I just wanted him to know that his kindness to me that day and his encouragement really gave me more resolve than ever to continue to follow my dream.

There were a lot of people in South Jersey who were looking at me when I'd say "Well, I'm going to be a blues guitarist" and they would look at me like "What the hell are you talking about?!" They didn't even know what that meant. Now, I have to say my parents were not like that. My father had B.B. King records and he had John Lee Hooker and he had T-Bone Walker and I heard the blues growing up, so my parents were always very supportive of me. But the other people like the teachers in my school and people like that-- they looked at me as if I was some kind of alien being and that I was doomed to failure!

But, B.B. gave me the resolve. He told me, he said "Follow your dream." I also know he said things that kind of crack me up when I look back. He said "Look, if you want to become a big, rich star by playing music, don't play the blues!" He said "That's not what it's about. The blues is something you play because you have to. You can't help it. It is what you have to do and it really chooses you." He added "It's almost like this deep, internal need that you have. But if you are just in music to make money, play a different kind of music!" That was some great advice. But when I was with John Mayall, I got to spend a lot of time with B.B. We became friends and I'll never forget... For instance, one time, I was walking through an airport in Stockholm. I had a layover there with John and we had like six hours or something and we were all just wandering around the airport. There was this empty gate and there were all these seats and there was one man sitting in the gate, sitting there reading a book and I looked and it was B.B. King!"

I went over and I said "Hello Mr. King. I'm Walter, I play with John Mayall" and he went "Oh, Hey Walter! How are you? Sit down!" And I sat there and, again, we talked for like hours and we hung out and laughed, told jokes and he was just the genuinely, sincere, beautiful man, who seemed to really love people. That was not an act that he put on. When I would say to him, "To me, you are the greatest of all time", he'd just say... "Oh no man, no man, I'm just a fellow trying to make a living playing the guitar", he used to tell me. What a great, great man.

He was the greatest blues musician ever in my estimation. But, even more than that, he was a great human being. I think that's his main legacy. The music is there, but for those people who got to know him and met him, his legacy is the humility and the gentleness and the kindness that he radiated and there's a lot of musicians out there that could learn from that and I wish there were more like that. He was a shining example of what a human being should be.

It's funny, I wish we had Skype 'cause I could show you--I'm wearing a B.B. King t-shirt as we speak! I just played at B.B. King's club in New York on Times Square and I bought myself a t-shirt and I'm wearing it as we speak! And, I have worn it at a couple of gigs, just to kind of 'fly the colours', you know. On this entire tour I've done a B.B. King tribute every night. And if you go on 'YouTube' and look up on this tour, it's called 'Say Goodbye to the Blues' and I start the song off. It's slow blues in a minor key and every night before I sing the song, I talk about B.B. and I dedicate it to him. On this tour, it's for B.B.

His legacy to me is: I try to emulate him when I'm going to meet the fans and meet people. If somebody comes up to me and says "Hey Walter Trout, I like your music", I think of what B.B.-- it's like--you know, how they say "What would Jesus do?" Well, I say "What would B.B. do?" How would he handle this situation? Here's a fan that wants to talk to me. And I know how he would do it and I try to be like that, because I was so inspired by that. I have time for people and he really showed me the way to be with my fans and friends. To me you've got B.B. King and then you've got everybody else. And as I said to my son, when my son Dylan was 10 or 11 years old and we opened for B.B. and B.B. picked my son up and put him on his lap and talked to him for like 20 minutes. And I said to Dylan after that "You know-- guys who do what I do for a living? That's the man who invented it".

He invented blues electric guitar as far as I'm concerned. And I said "So Dylan, the rest of your life, I want you to remember that you sat on that man's lap and talked to him when you were a kid and he was not only the greatest blues man of all time, but he's an icon. He's a giant in the history of this, he is a giant." And Dylan looked at me and said "I understand that dad, but when you meet him, he's just like a friendly neighbour." To this day, my son Dylan has a bunch of photos of B.B. King framed and up on the wall in his bedroom. Other kids have, however, Eminem or Lady Gaga on their wall. My son has pictures of B.B. King.

I did a show at the Royal Albert Hall recently and I did a tribute to B.B. that night. That's the first song I did. I did 'Say Goodbye to the Blues' and I dedicated to B.B. King. I appreciate what you are doing for B.B's memory.

Walter Trout
August 14, 2015

(Photo: Marie Trout)

> " ... To me you've got B.B. King and then you've got everybody else. And as I said to my son ... 'You know-- guys who do what I do for a living? That's the man who invented it". He invented blues electric guitar as far as I'm concerned ... the rest of your life, I want you to remember that you sat on that man's lap and talked to him ... and he was not only the greatest blues man of all time ... he's an icon .. he is a giant.'"

Walter Trout

Keb Mo

Anytime I would cross paths with B.B. King, it was "always" a very special event. I first met B.B. in the early 70's, when a member of the "Papa John Creach" Band. The bill was; Creach, The Average White Band and of course "B.B. King". That was my first time seeing him live. He was amazing.

Throughout my adult life, I encountered the King at various concerts. He always delivered. In the mid-nineties, I met B.B. at a fundraiser in Universal City, in Los Angeles, California. That was the first time I really saw him for who he really was: "The King". He walked in with an aura of royalty, grace and class I had never seen. At that moment, I saw what it meant to wear the crown of "King of the Blues".

**Keb Mo
August 20, 2015**

(Photo: Charley Gallay/Getty Images for Thelonious Monk Institute)

(Photo: Charley Gallay/Getty Images for Thelonious Monk Institute)

Anytime I would cross paths with B.B. King, it was "always" a very special event.

I first met B.B. in the early 70's while a member of the "Papa John Creach" band. The bill was, Creach, the "Average White Band" and of course "B.B. King". That was my first time seeing him live. He was amazing.

Throughout my adult life I encountered the King at various concerts. He always delivered. In the mid nineties I met B.B. at a fundraiser in Universal City, in Los Angeles, CA. That was the first time I really saw him for who he really was "The King". He walked in with an aura of Royalty, Grace and Class I had never seen. At that moment I saw what it meant to wear the crown of "King of the Blues".

Keb Mo

Keb Mo handwritten tribute to B.B., August 2015

Regi Richards

I became a member of the B.B. King Band on August 3, 2002. My first gig was Eugene, Oregon at a festival of which I can't recall the name. I played bass for Mr. King until he discontinued performing in October of 2014. With all of those years working for and performing with a Blues Icon, Music Legend and Ambassador to the World it is still difficult to word the experience as anything short of privileged, honored and fortunate.

Mr. King was many things through my eyes. All of those were positive and, in many ways, of contrast. Here are some examples: He was a rich man and could have been selfish, but he was filled with compassion and selflessness. He was a Bluesman but had an affinity and appreciation for other genres of music. He traveled and moved effortlessly through the world but was often still and accessible. He, at times, had every reason to frown but you rarely caught him without a smile and a kind word.

Mr. King was and will always be, one of the most generous, patient, kind, talented, positive and unique people I've had the honor of knowing and working with. It is because of my time with Mr. King that I consider myself truly, absolutely and uncompromisingly privileged...

With all love, appreciation and respect, Thank you Mr. King.

Regi "Youngblood" Richards
August 21, 2015

(Las Vegas Review Journal)

LAS VEGAS PAYS TRIBUTE TO B.B. KING

On Friday May 22, 2015 hundreds of people lined up in front of Palms South Mortuary in Las Vegas to pay their respects and say goodbye to B.B., the "King of Blues" before he was laid to rest in Mississippi. Fans arrived early, forming a long line throughout the day. A speaker played blues music outside as some mourners danced and sang, both alone and together. Many wore t-shirts with B.B. King's iconic image. Georgia Jackson who had traveled from San Francisco to pay her respects expressed very beautifully the sentiment felt by so many others:

> "I have memories...You know, it's life. I grew up with him. I lived that life... 'The Thrill is Gone,'Why I Sing the Blues'... all those songs...I lived that life." [74]

The following day, on Saturday, May 23, tears, cheers and a standing ovation marked private B.B. King memorial services held for friends and family near the Las Vegas Strip. Two Lucille guitars stood amidst beautiful floral arrangements with a tapestry showing B.B. playing his guitar in loving reverie. Several of his adult children and grandchildren expressed loving tributes during the intimate two-hour service.

> "For everyone else, he was a legend," his granddaughter said, "But for us, he was love." [75]

His grandson Leonard King Jr. recalled the sentiment shared by so many others who knew the blues legend,

"His humility was almost as legendary as his music." [76]

B.B. King classics were sung acapella during the service. Rock superstars Carlos Santana, Richie Sambora, Tony Coleman, King's onstage drummer for 37 years, and longtime manager Laverne Toney were also among 300 mourners in attendance at this invitational only service. Santana said to one reporter that B.B. had greatly inspired his own career,

"I am deeply saddened by the passing of 'The Chairman of the Board,' B.B. King. He is now on the other side with Bob Marley, John Coltrane, Miles Davis and many others. His one-of-a-kind sound was an inspiration to an entire generation of musicians, including myself. He will be missed by millions of fans and by countless musicians. I would like to extend my sincerest condolences to the King family. May he rest in eternal peace." [77]

Like Santana, B.B. played many times in Las Vegas. His early introduction to Las Vegas was facilitated during the 70's by another legendary "Chairman of the Board" who expressed great respect and admiration for B.B.'s artistry – the famed crooner Frank Sinatra. Many years later, B.B. would open his own B.B. King Blues Club at the Mirage Hotel on the Strip.

(B.B. King at the Mirage)

Early Clover

Early Clover, Las Vegas

Another Las Vegas showroom legend who broke showroom records during his ten year engagement at the Sahara Hotel is Early Clover, lead singer for the Cornell Gunter Coasters. He has been entertaining for 26 years at the Desert Inn, Flamingo, Hilton and other major hotels on the Strip. In a recent telephone interview, he remembered fondly the time he spent with B.B. King after opening for him several times both in Las Vegas and other venues. B.B. was not only a man he was proud to call his friend, but also a lifetime inspiration and mentor,

> "I first fell in love with the guitar and learned to play music because of B.B. King. When I first heard him sing I was about six years old. My dad and my older brother used to sit under the tree in our front yard in Georgia playing B.B. King songs over and over again. My dad would play the harmonica and my brother would play the guitar. B.B.'s big hit that year was 'Sweet Sixteen'. They would play that song together and people would pass by and stop to listen. I struggled to learn that song but at six years old a real guitar was too big for me. So my dad got me a smaller guitar with plastic strings. I didn't like it because it didn't sound like his did, so I made my own guitar out of a two by four and some hay strings. I went slamming away on that guitar singing 'Sweet Sixteen' and finally annoyed my father so much that he found me a small 'real' guitar. So by eight years

old I could finally play that complete song and then I started to learn his other songs.

We had also a phonograph at the time that played 78s and 45s and 33 LPs-- and when we had a Fish Fry, we would all sit around it and play and sing. It was either B.B. or Bobby Blue Bland all the time! B.B. King became for our family what I would call our household musician when I was coming up. At that time, the distinct sounds of B.B. King differed from other blues players. He was always different from the others. Something about his technique... when B.B. played he made the guitar say things that he couldn't say with words himself. The guitar would...I would say it had such meaning!

Some people say "blues music is gospel music played backwards". I beg to differ. I say that blues shakes the soul. Shakes the soul up-- and stirs it! B.B. King was the Master of Blues. Every single note B.B. played would emulate something he would feel or he would be saying, but he was saying all of it through that guitar!

When I first met B.B. King I was opening for him at the Desert Inn in the mid to late 90s. By that time I had already performed with many superstars but B.B. King was one of the most down to earth people of everyone I've ever known. How open he was to us and how humble he was. He was a superstar, so he really didn't even need to talk to us. You would think a man of such status, would be stuck up, but not B.B. King! Where some might say that talking was wasting his time B.B. would say, 'Let's talk ...'

We performed in the same arenas together as time went on and each time we shared the stage, after that night, B.B. would always acknowledge me by saying, 'Hello my friend' ... and he always knew and remembered my name. He said once that I had such a unique name. 'That's a real deep South kind a name!' he said.

He was such a wonderful and sometimes humorous person whom I'd like to call a friend. He was always positive and, although he was a perfectionist, to my knowledge, he treated his band with the utmost respect. I'm glad I got a chance to meet and share the stage with the man and his guitar--Mr. B.B King! I still follow one of his most treasured advices for me:

'The moment you forget where you come from, you won't know where you're going.'"

Early Clover
Lead singer of The Cornell Gunter Coasters
August 25, 2015

B.B. King Blues Club Sign

Leonard King
Fresh Prince of the Blues

I am one of the oldest grandsons of the man you all know of as B.B. King. Personally, I have had many honors in my lifetime, most of them achieved in relative anonymity, outside of the radiance of my legendary grandfather. However, to be asked to write something—anything—on his behalf is humbling and an opportunity that I could not let slip by. It is my honor to be able to have the opportunity to write these words, not just for me, but for all of the King grandchildren. I am almost positive that he is smiling down upon me as I share my words with you. So many thanks to Richard Booth for asking me to add on to an already grand legacy. I truly hope I am able to do my grandfather's memory a great justice and service.

I excogitated (I got my love of big words from my grandfather who always encouraged my passion for reading and knowledge) long and hard on what to write. I have written an almost 400 page novel, yet writing a few words for someone who I loved and admired so dearly was not as simple as I thought it would be. In a few words I cannot possibly convey all that this man has meant to me or the profound effect he has had on my life. And not just to me, but also the rest of his family. He was our own true-to-life legend and hero. And as part of his family we got to see a more personal side of him: his humanness.

I was fortunate to be able to spend some personal quality time with my grandfather at a young age when I moved to Las Vegas to live with my own father. I was about eight years old and it was during this time that I really got to know him, although I had a lot of life to live and maturing to do before I would be able to understand him. I have wonderful memories of that time, when I was the only young child on his huge Alta Dr. estate. In the twenty four hours it had taken us to drive from Arkansas to Las Vegas I had gone from a two bedroom apartment that was home to eight inhabitants to a five bedroom home, even more bathrooms, with a swimming pool and tennis court. I was the

Leonard King showing his first novel "The Lying Tree" to his beloved grandfather, B.B. King. (photo courtesy of Leonard King)

original Fresh Prince of Las Vegas. Most of the time my grandfather was on the road and the only people in his home would be myself, my father, his faithful secretary Miss Laverne, who was working out of the house at the time, and his three dogs, King, Prince, and Duke.

He was on the road a lot, but when he did come home, however, he and I spent a lot of quality time together. He would take me out on an impromptu ride in his favorite car, a red and white El Camino, when he just wanted to get out of the house. It was not the prettiest nor fanciest car in the world, but it was his pride and joy. For those who are unfamiliar with El Caminos, they looked like a hybrid of a station wagon and small pick-up truck. It seated three people in the cab with the bench seats and could carry any number of people on the open back, depending on how daring they would be. He could have easily afforded a fancier car, and he actually did own another, but his preference was that El Camino. I don't recall if there was ever a particular destination we had. I was just happy to be in his presence. I did not realize at the time how lucky I actually was to be able to spend quality time with him. I would not realize that until I was much older and more aware of who he was not just to me but to the world. The excited feeling that never left me, even when I had aged into my forties with children of my own I would still get excited to see him. My time with him always seemed too short.

Or other times he would just have me around in his large cluttered master bedroom so he could laugh at the things I would say. He always did have an affection for kids who were outspoken, of which I definitely was. He was a kid at heart himself, and other than his three good friends Marvin, Reese, and Alice Mae, although I was the youngest I may have also been his best friend at the time.

We had a very close relationship which continued until the day he passed away. He was as proud of me and my ordinary accomplishments as I was of him and his legendary status. He was a huge advocate of post-education, an opportunity that he had not been afforded (or could even fathom) when he was younger. He offered to all of his grandkids and children the same thing: his full financial support to any college of their choice, which I accepted. His word was as true as his plucks on his guitar strings. He supported me in obtaining my Bachelors in Electrical Engineering and then surprised me and the rest of my family and friends when he showed up unannounced at my graduation. My grandfather, B.B. King, King of the Blues, legend, superstar, at the age of 72 years, drove alone from Memphis, TN to Jonesboro, Arkansas, which is an hour plus ride with no traffic, in the era of no GPS guides, to personally see me get my degree. I almost fell to my knees when I saw him walk up to me with a proud, smug smile on his face. I am getting chills right simply writing about it. But that was how close our relationship was. He made sure his very busy schedule allowed him that day off to see me graduate from college.

My grandfather's humility was almost as legendary and well known as his music. He never bragged or boasted about what he did or who he was. Every kind word or compliment he was given was received with the same genuine graciousness (hands clasped over his heart and a thank you), as if he hadn't heard it a thousand times before. But there was one thing he was quite proud of. There was one thing which he would proclaim to his audiences and fans every time he was given the chance. And that was that he was a grandfather.

He would be surrounded by a throng of fans, or even on stage, but when he caught a glimpse of one of his grandchildren he would stop what he was doing and interrupt his show to call us over so he could tell the audience of whoever was listening who we were. He was the star, yet he wanted to shine some of his light on us.

My grandfather's time was scarce. He was most accessible to his family when he was traveling. Whenever the venue in which he was playing was in close proximity to where I resided we would go to see him. These were happy moments for him as well as for me and my family. He would lose sleep and rest to entertain everyone who came out to see him. He would even take the time to see everyone individually if he could manage it. He knew every one of his grandchildren on a personal level. He knew what we were doing in life and he cared enough to inquire as to our well being when he could. He was busy, but never too busy. He was hard to contact at times, but he still expected us to persist and find a way to get in touch. The times that he called me unexpectedly, such as Christmas Day a few years ago, are moments which I will cherish until my dying day.

He was not your everyday grandfather. Because he simply was not your typical man. He could not attend recreational activities, most graduations, keep us overnight, or cater to us like he wanted to. But he did what he could, the best he could. He gave advice, support, and lectures, whether we asked for the latter or not. He taught me to look people in the eyes when you talk to them. He taught me to always give a firm handshake. He asked all of his grandchildren to dress respectably and impeccably, as to always look professional, and to always respect women. That's what fathers and grandfathers do, no matter where they are or what they are doing.

The point I am trying to pass on to all, because I truly want everyone in the world to know it, is what my grandfather always told us with his words and showed with his actions: he was our grandfather, first and foremost, who just happened to be B.B. King.

Leonard King
September 5, 2015

B.B. King RPM promo photo (Collection of Richard Booth)

Above we see B.B. – the vibrant young man ... a blossoming career ... And on following page, a loving patriarch, years later ... the nurturing touch of the "King's" incredible hands ...   R.B.

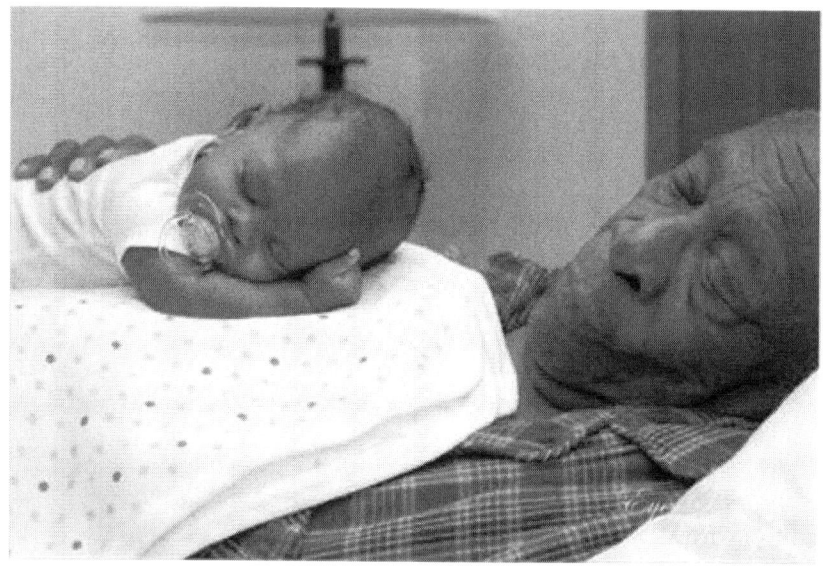

B.B. and his Great Grandson (Photo courtesy of Leonard King)

"I did not realize at the time how lucky I actually was to be able to spend quality time with him. I would not realize that until I was much older and more aware of who he was not just to me but to the world. The excited feeling that never left me, even when I had aged into my forties with children of my own I would still get excited to see him. My time with him always seemed too short." (Leonard King)

(Photo courtesy of Rita King)

Rita King pictured here with her father, B.B. King. Rita spent many joyful hours traveling alongside her father and has captured these lovingly in her book "On the Road with My Dad the King of the Blues, Mr. B.B. King". Her book contains a rare collection of never seen before personal photos and stories.

Rita's Tribute to her father Mr. Riley B.B. King

To My Father the Commander in Chief, Mr. Riley AKA B.B. King:

Thank you for empowering me to use the DNA you gave me.

Being *On the Road* with you has been a part of the divine order.

I feel the love the world feels for you. People accept me for me.

Dad...you have mesmerized your audience throughout the world...

Today, yesterday, and every day that there is breath

The Universe will honor you by celebrating the birth of a dream come true with Lucille. You two are two peas in a pod.

Because of your due diligence, the sounds of B.B. King can be heard in the new space habitats throughout the galaxies.

Not only has your music inspired and influenced the American culture...

You have encouraged young guitarists to play just like you!

Dad you are my love, you are my laughter, you are my hanky to wipe away my tears, which is just the joy and job of a truly wonderful father.

Dad, you are free now. The chains and things are no more.

I will make sure that your grave is kept clean.

Again, thank you for falling in love with my mother and making me.

I love and miss you muchly,

Your daughter,

Rita King
September 7, 2015

B.B.'s Grammy Award with Eric Clapton for 'Riding with the King', 2000

B.B. King Handprints and signature at 'Billy Bob's', Fort Worth, Texas, 25/09/04 (Photo: Richard Booth)

B.B. King autograph (Collection of Richard Booth)

AWARDS

B.B. King has received a phenomenal amount of recognition worldwide over his amazing career. Below is a complete list of the awards and accolades throughout the years.

Honorary Doctorates

2007	Brown University (Providence, Rhode Island) (D. Music)
1990	Rhodes College (Memphis) (D. Fine Arts)
1982	Berklee College of Music (Boston) (D. Music)
1977	Yale University (D. Music)
1973	Tougaloo College (Mississippi) (L.H.D)

Honorariums

2008	The keys to the city of Portland, Maine
2004	Polar Music Prize – The Royal Swedish Academy of Music
1995	Kennedy Center Honours
1991	National Award of Distinction – University of Mississippi
1991	National Heritage Fellowship – National Endowment of the Arts
1990	Presidential Medal of the Arts, Presented by President George Bush

Founding Member, John F. Kennedy Performing Arts Center
Co-founder, Foundation for the Advancement of Inmate Recreation and Rehabilitation (F.A.I.R.R.)

Presidential Medal of Freedom

2006 Presidential Medal of Freedom

W.C. Handy Awards (Blues Foundation)

2002	Entertainer of the Year
2001	Contemporary Album of the Year
2001	Entertainer of the Year

2000	Entertainer of the Year
1999	Entertainer of the Year
1999	Contemporary Album of the Year
1994	Contemporary Album of the Year
1981	Entertainer of the Year
1991	Blues Band of the Year – The B.B. King Orchestra
1988	Keeping the Blues Alive (Radio) – The B.B. King Radio Hour
1987	Keeping the Blues Alive (Radio) – The B.B. King Radio Hour
1985	Hall of Fame Classics of Blues Recordings (Single Recording, Including Album Tracks)
1983	Hall of Fame Classics of Blues Recordings (Albums) – Live at the Regal 'The Thrill Is Gone'

MTV Video Music Awards

1988/89	Best Video from a Film, 'When Loves Comes To Town' from Rattle & Hum, U2 with B.B. King

NAACP Image Awards

1993	Best Blues Artist
1981	Best Blues Artist
1975	Best Blues Artist

National Association for Campus Activities Awards

1986	Blues Act of the Year

NATRA Golden Mike Award

1974	Best Blues Singer of the Year
1969	Best Blues Singer of the Year

French Academie du Jazz Award

1969		Best Album of the Year, Lucille

Grammy Awards

2014		Grammy Hall of Fame Award
2009		Best Traditional Blues Album
2006		Grammy Hall of Fame Award
2006		Best Traditional Blues Album
2004		Grammy Hall of Fame Award
2003		Best Traditional Blues Album
2002		Entertainer of the Year

2001		Best Traditional Blues Album
		Riding With The King

2000		Best Pop Collaboration with Vocals, Is You Is, Or Is You Ain't (My Baby), B.B. King & Dr. John

		Best Traditional Blues Album, Blues on the Bayou

1993		Best Traditional Blues Recording,
		Blues Summit

1991		Best Traditional Blues Recording,
		Live at the Apollo

1990		Best Traditional Blues Recording,
		Live at San Quentin

1985		Best Traditional Blues Recording,
		'My Guitar Sing the Blues', a track from
		Six Silver Strings

1983		Best Traditional Blues Recording,
		Blues & Jazz

1981		Best Ethnic or Traditional Recording,
		There Must Be A Better World Somewhere

1970 Best Rhythm & Blues Vocal Performance, Male, 'The Thrill Is Gone'

1970 Best Album Cover, An Art Director's Award, Indianola Mississippi Seeds

Halls Of Fame

1995 Performance Magazine touring Hall of Fame

1987 Rock and Roll Hall of Fame

1984 Blues Hall of Fame

1980 Blues Foundation Hall of Fame

Lifetime Achievement Awards

1998 MOBO award Lifetime Achievement
1991 The Orville H. Gibson Lifetime Achievement Award (Gibson Guitar)

1990 Songwriter's Hall of Fame, Lifetime Achievement Award

1987 Grammy Awards Lifetime Achievement Award

Humanitarian Awards

1973 B'Nai Brith Humanitarian Award, Music and Performance Lodge of New York

Walks of Fame

1991 Hollywood Walk of Fame
    (Between Milton Berle and Vivian Leigh)

1989 Amsterdam (Holland) Walk of Fame

1989 Rock Walk

Downbeat

1995	Blues Group (International Critics Poll)
1994	Blues Album of the Year (Blues Summit) (International Critics Poll)
1994	Blues Artist of the Year (International Critics Poll)
1994	Blues Group (International Critics Poll)
1994	Blues / Soul / R&B Album of the Year (Blues Summit) (Reader Poll)
1994	Blues / Soul / R&B Musician of the Year (Readers Poll)
1994	Blues / Soul / R&B Group of the Year (Readers Poll)
1993	Blues Artist of the Year International Critics Poll
1993	Blues Group (International Critics Poll)
1993	Blues / Soul / R&B Musician of the Year (Readers Poll)
1993	Blues / Soul / R&B Group of the Year (Readers Poll)
1992	Blues Group (International Critics Poll)
1992	Blues Artist of the Year (International Critics Poll)
1991	Blues Artist of the Year (International Critics Poll)
1991	Blues / Soul / R&B Musician of the Year (Readers Poll)
1990	Blues / Soul / R&B Musician of the Year (Readers Poll)
1975	Best Rock / Pop / Blues Group (International Critics Poll)
1974	Best Rock / Pop / Blues Group (International Critics Poll)

1973	Best Rock / Pop / Blues Group (International Critics Poll)
1972	Best Rock / Pop / Blues Group (International Critics Poll)
1971	Best Rock / Pop / Blues Group (International Critics Poll)
1970	Best Rock / Pop / Blues Group (International Critics Poll)

Ebony Magazine

1975	Best Blues Album, To Know You Is To Love You
1975	Best Blues Instrumentalist
1975	Best Male Blues Singer
1974	Best Blues Album, Live at the Regal
1974	Best Blues Instrumentalist
1974	Best Male Blues Singer
1974	Blues Hall of Fame

Guitar Player Magazine

1974	Blues Guitarist of the Year
1973	Blues Guitarist of the Year
1972	Blues Guitarist of the Year
1971	Blues Guitarist of the Year
1970	Blues Guitarist of the Year

Performance Magazine Readers Poll

1988	Blues Act of the Year
1987	Blues Act of the Year
1985	Blues Act of the Year

Melody Maker

1973   Best Blues Artist of the Year (World Section)

Blues Unlimited

1973   Best Blues Guitarist

Jazz & Pop

1967   Best Male Jazz Singer of the Year

B.B. King WDIA portrait

B.B. back again at the Apollo Theatre in Manchester, England 2011

Photos: Richard Booth

B.B. AND THE AUTHOR IN PARIS

LUCILLE

No tribute to B.B. King would be complete without some words regarding the instrument that provided the amazing music from B.B.'s finger tips-- his one true love--his guitar, Lucille. There have been approximately twenty guitars that B.B. King has called Lucille (the name he originally gave to his own guitar after the fire incident at the dance hall in Twist, Arkansas, 1949). That specific guitar was a Gibson L-30: the first Lucille! Made between 1935 and 1943, the Gibson L-30 was one of Gibson's budget models, although that guitar would certainly be worth a small fortune today! It was a small bodied, non-cutaway model with a flat back. It featured a simple trapeze tailpiece, pickguard, an adjustable bridge, single bound body (front and back) and single dot fingerboard markers. Earlier models had black bodies and later versions a dark mahogany back and sides with a dark sunburst top. The model was discontinued in 1943.

Lucille Number Two was a Gibson ES-5. As B.B.'s earnings grew, he turned his attention to more upmarket Gibson models. This was one of Gibson's more versatile and good-looking guitars. The ES-5 was first released in 1949 with three P-90 pickups. B.B.'s was the early version that did not have the more complicated switching later featured on models from the 1955-1960 period. It was released in both blonde and sunburst body finishes. B.B. had the blonde model with three volume controls below the raised black pickguard and a single tone pot adjacent to the rounded Venetian cutaway. The three P-90 pickups were set into the laminated maple top with an adjustable bridge, trapeze tailpiece and two beautifully cut f-holes. This guitar model was discontinued in 1960.

(Photo: AP)

After B.B.'s first hit single 'Three O'Clock Blues' was released in 1951, he began using Gibson's amazing budget ES-125. It had a single P-90 neck pickup and the effects of this feature can be heard on the songs clearly. The guitar was 16.25 inches wide and 3.5 inches thick with no cutaway. It had a bound top and back with a lovely tortoise shell pickguard, raised diamond' trapeze tailpiece, single-bound' top and back with carried dot fingerboard inlays. It was only available in a dark sunburst finish. It was discontinued in 1970.

Next, B.B. chose a thinner archtop in the Gibson Byrdland model, which was perceived to be top of the line at the time. These were released in 1955, with slimmer bodies, more refined specifications and a shorter scale length. This model would be nicknamed the 'Byrdland' as it was endorsed by jazz players: Billy Byrd and Hank Garland. It was available in both blonde or sunburst models, with a 17 inch wide body that was only 2.25 inches deep. It also featured an ebony fingerboard with block pearl inlays.

As the electric guitar market developed and redefined itself during the 1950's, B.B. was on a constant search for the 'right' guitar that would suit his style of playing. He spent time playing Fender's new Esquire, a single pickup Telecaster, which became a good sounding model for some blues guitarists. Even though it had a single coil pickup, the Esquire's clever switching allowed for fat bass tones as well as sharp ones, plus a good sound in the middle. B.B.'s model is an early pre-1950 model, as its 12th fret dots are closer together than later versions. The black pickguard on his Esquire guitar was changed to feature a white one in 1954 and the maple neck changed to that of a dark rosewood fingerboard in 1959.

The next model B.B. would favour was the Gibson ES-175. This model has never been discontinued and is a firm favourite with Jazz guitarists. It was first released in 1949 with blonde or tobacco sunburst finishes, a Florentine pointed cutaway and double parallelogram fingerboard markers. It also featured a lovely white neck and body binding. The early models featured a single P-90 pickup, changing to two by 1953. The body of the guitar was laminated maple as this kept the price down and made it less susceptible to the changes of the climate and feedback when played. In 1957-58, the ES-175 was the first model to feature the new Gibson humbucker pickup. B.B. is pictured with this model on the 1959 album release 'B.B. King Wails'.

In 1958, Gibson developed the first semi-solid model with the ES-300 series. The 'standard' series was the ES-355, the 'deluxe 'stereo' ES-345, complete with gold hardware and six position Varitone switch, and the 'custom' level ES-355, which also featured stereo with Varitone, but had multiple bindings, ebony fingerboard with pearl inlay blocks and a vibrato tailpiece. These apparent semi-acoustic guitars actually had a fully solid centre section that gave huge tone and fantastic versatility. They also had the new humbucker pickups, were light in weight, and they played fantastic. B.B. was often pictured with the Bigsbsy vibrato tailpiece and, although it suited him as a player, he felt he needed something that looked more special. B.B. really thought he had finally found the guitar that suited him the best. The Gibson ES-355 had everything that he needed in a guitar. It played great, it looked fantastic and had the controls and versatility his style of playing needed and demanded. It also allowed for sweet tones and more powerful ringing tones that perfectly complimented his playing and his love for more 'vocal' tones. It featured a six-way Varitone switch that offered an array of different sounds over and above Gibson's usual sound. These new sounds can be heard dramatically on 'The Thrill is Gone', where B.B. allowed listeners to hear the full sounds of his guitar.

After B.B. had been playing the ES-355 guitars exclusively for over twenty years, in 1980, Gibson approached him to create his own exclusive 'Lucille' model. His model featured personalised pearl inlays. B.B. also requested that Gibson remove the f-holes because at high volume and in close standing to an amp, those can give acoustic feedback. When playing, B.B. often had put a cloth in his regular ES-355 f-holes to stop this unwanted feedback from occurring. He also included the Schaller TP-6 fine tuning tailpiece, which really set off the guitar both in terms of playability and look. The guitar is available in both B.B.'s preferred ebony finish and in cherry red. In 2005 for B.B.'s 80th birthday, Gibson built a small run of 80th Birthday Lucille's. They presented B.B. with the prototype model as his own special anniversary gift. The guitar was later stolen from B.B., but it was found by a person in a pawn store who returned it to him straight away!

The Gibson version of the Lucille is a high-end priced instrument, yet B.B. had always said that his music is for everyone, not for just an exclusive few. In response, Gibson's sister brand Epiphone released a more affordable version of 'Lucille' which still looks amazing. It features a laminated maple body with glued-in maple neck, a bound rosewood fingerboard and multi-bound body and headstock. It has both stereo and mono outputs, plus a six-way Varitone switch and two Classic Alnico humbucker pickups and a TP-6 fine tuning tailpiece. The guitar also has a beautiful 'Lucille' logo inlaid into the head of the guitar, a gold plated 'B.B. King' truss rod cover, and three-a-side Grover tuners. All the hardware is also finished in gold.

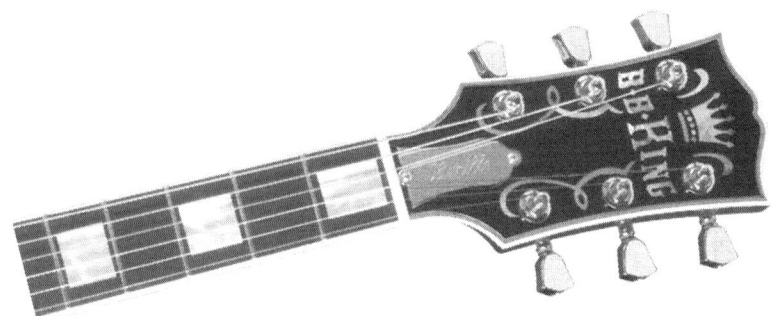

B.B. King's Gibson Headstock (Photo: Gibson)

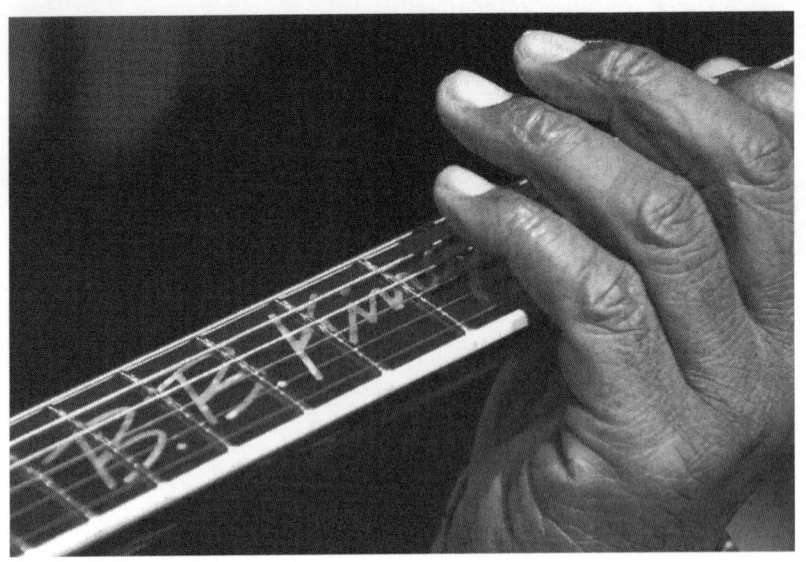

(Photo: AFP/Getty Images)

B.B. King Gibson Lucille (Photo: Gibson)

(Photo: AP)

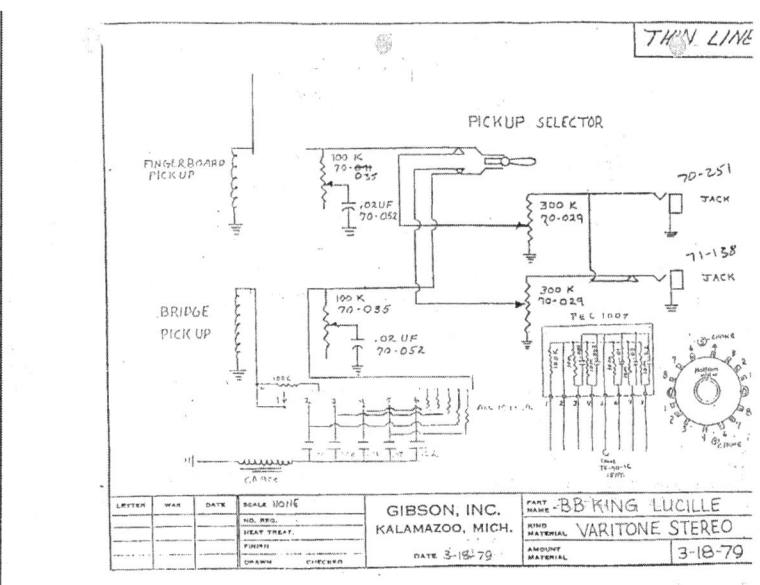
(Photo: Gibson)

BB King Guitar picks used throughout the years
(Collection of Richard Booth)

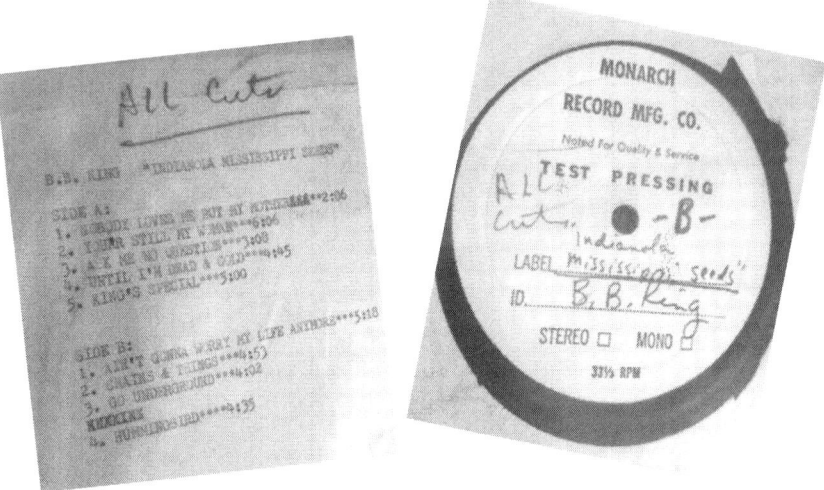

Original RPM "78 and record test pressing
(Collection of Richard Booth)

DISCOGRAPHY

A complete listing (apologies if I left anything out!) of B.B. King's songs and albums recorded throughout his career. I have left out many compilation albums from recent years and concentrated on the main releases and important hits packages.

1949	Bullet 309 (8/49)	Miss Martha King When Your Baby Packs Up and Goes
	Bullet 315 (10/49)	Got the Blues Take a swing
1950	RPM 304 (9/50)	Mistreated Woman B.B's Boogie
	RPM 311 (12/50)	The Other Night Blues Walkin' and Cryin'
1951	RPM 318 (3/51)	My Baby's Gone Don't You Want a Man Like Me?
	RPM 323 (6/51)	B.B's Blues She's Dynamite
	RPM 330 (8/51)	She's a Mean Woman Hard Working Woman
	RPM 339 (12/51)	Three O'Clock Blues That Ain't the Way to Do It

RPM 348 (4/52)   She Don't Move Me No More
                  Fine Looking Woman

From 1951 sessions, released later on compilation albums:
                  A New Way of Driving
                  Questionnaire Blues
                  I Got a Girl Who Lives Up On The Hill

1952 RPM 355 (5/52)   Shake It Up and Go
                            (It's) My Own Fault Darling

          RPM 360 (7/52)   Gotta Find My Baby
                            Some Day Somewhere

          RPM 363 (8/52)   You Know I Love You (R&B #1 – 1952)
                            You Didn't Want Me

          RPM 374 (12/52)   Story from My Heart and Soul (R&B #9 – 1952)
                            Boogie Woogie Woman

          RPM 380 (3/53)   Woke Up This Morning (My Baby She Was Gone) (R&B # 3 – 1953)
                            Don't Have to Cry (Past Day)

From 1952 sessions, released later on compilation albums:
                  Low Down Dirty Baby
                  I'm So Glad
                  Pray for You

1953 RPM 386 (6/53)   Please Love Me (R&B #1–1953)
                            Highway Bound
                            Please Hurry Home (R&B # 4 – 1953)
                            Neighborhood Affair

          RPM 395 (12/53)   Blind Love
                            Why Did You Leave Me

          RPM 403 (2/54)   Praying to the Lord
                            Please Help Me

Unissued sides recorded for Don Robey's Peacock label:
                  Remember Me
                  What a Difference

    I Don't Believe It
    I Can't Put You Down
    I Did Everything I Could
    I've Learned My Lesson
     Come On Baby Take a Swing with Me
    (I Want You to) Love Me

1954   RPM 408 (4/54)   I Love You Baby
                                     The Woman I Love

         RPM 411 (6/54)   Don't You Want a Man Like Me
                                     Everything I Do Is Wrong

         RPM 412 (7/54)   When My Heart Beats Like a Hammer
                                     (R&B # 8 – 1954)
                                     Bye! Bye! Baby

         RPM 416 (10/54)   You Upset Me Baby (R&B #1–1954)
                                     Whole Lot of Love (R&B #8 – 1954)

From 1954 sessions, released later on compilation albums:
                          Please Remember Me

1955   RPM 421 (1/55)   Every Day (I Have the Blues)
                                     (R&B #8 – 1955)
                                     Sneakin' Around (with You)
                                     (R&B #14 – 1955)

         RPM 425 (4/55)   Lonely and Blue
                                     Jump With You Baby

         RPM 430 (7/55)   I'm in Love
                                     Shut Your Mouth

         RPM 435 (8/55)   Talking the Blues
                                     Boogie Rock

         RPM 437 (9/55)   Ten Long Years (I Had a Woman)
                                     (R&B #9 – 1955)
                                     What Can I Do (Just Sing the Blues)

         RPM 450 (12/55)   I'm Cracking Up Over You
                                     Ruby Lee

From 1955 sessions, released later on compilation albums or Kent 45's:
        I Was Blind
        Baby Look at You

1956   RPM 457 (3/56)   Did You Ever Love a Woman
                               Let's Do The Boogie

        RPM 459 (4/56)   Dark Is The Night Pt. 1
                               Dark Is The Night Pt. 2

        RPM 468 (7/56)   Sweet Little Angel (R&B #3 – 1956)
                               Bad Luck (R&B #6 – 1956)

        RPM 479 (11/56)   On My Word of Honour
                               (R&B #3 – 1956)

From 1956 sessions, released later on compilation albums:
        Why I Sing the Blues

1957   RPM 486 (2/57)   Early in the Morning
                                 You Don't Know

        RPM 490 (3/57)   You Can't Fool My Heart
                               How Do I Love You

        RPM 492 (4/57)   I Want to Get Married
                               (R&B #4 – 1957)
                               Troubles Troubles Troubles
                               (R&B #13 – 1957)

        RPM 494 (6/57)   Be Careful With a Fool
                               (Hot #95 – 1957)
                               (I'm Gonna) Quit My Baby

        RPM 498 (9/57)   I Need You So Bad (Hot #85 – 1957)
                               I Wonder

        RPM 501 (11/57)   The Key to My Kingdom
                               My Heart Belongs to You

From 1957 sessions, released later on Kent 45s and/or compilation albums:
        I Stay in the Mood (R&B #45 – 1966 on Kent 450)
        Bad Breaks

1958   Kent 301 (3/58)   Why Do Everything Happen to Me
Kent 301 (3/58)   You Know I Go for You

Kent 307 (7/58)   Don't Look Now, But I've Got the Blues
Days of Old

Kent 315 (10/58)   Please Accept My Love (R&B #9 – 1958)
You've Been an Angel (R&B # 16 – 1958)

Kent 317 (2/59)   I Am
Worry Worry

Kent 319 (3/59)   Come by Here
The Fool (A Fool Too Long)

Kent 325 (6/59)   A Longley Lover's Pleas
The Woman I Love (R&B #31 & Hot # 94 – 1968, on Kent 492)

From 1958 sessions, released later on compilations albums:
Blues for Me (Groovin' Twist)
Looking the World Over
In the Middle of an Island
String Bean
I Love You So

Unissued sides recorded for Chess, released later on compilation albums:
Don't Keep Me Waiting
Recession Blues
Tickle Britches
Don't Break Your Promise

1959   Kent 327 (7/59)   Time to Say Goodbye
Every Day I Have the Blues (with members of the Count Basie Band)

Kent 329 (8/59)   Mean Ole Frisco
Sugar Mama

Kent 330 (10/59)	Sweet Sixteen Pt.1 (R&B #2 – 1960) Sweet Sixteen Pt.2
Kent 333	(I've) Got a Right to Love My Baby (R&B #8 1960) My Own Fault (or) Dry Bones
Kent 346	Partin' Time (R&B #8 – 1960) Good Man Gone Bad
Kent 350	Walking Doctor Bill (R&B#23–1960) You've Done Lost Your Good Thing Now
Kent 351	Things Are Not the Same Fish' After Me (Catfish Blues)
Kent 353	Get Out of Here Bad Luck Soul
Kent 358	Hold That Train Understand
Kent 360	Peace of Mind (R&B #7 – 1961) Someday (R&B #16 – 1961)
Kent 362	Bad Case of Love You're Breaking My Heart
Kent 365	Lonely My Sometime Baby (R&B #27– 1962)
Kent 372	Gonna Miss You Around Here (R&B #17 – 1962) Hully Gully (Twist)
Kent 373	Mashed Potato Time Three O'Clock Stomp
Kent 381	Mashing the Popeye Tell Me Baby

Kent 383	When My Heart Beats Like a Hammer Going Down Slow
Kent 386	Three O'Clock Blues Your Letter
Kent 387	Christmas Celebration Easy Listening (Blues)
Kent 388	Whole Lot of Lovin' Down Now
Kent 389	Trouble in Mind Long Nights
Kent 390	My Reward The Road I Travel
Kent 391	The Letter You Better Know
Kent 393	Rock Me Baby (Hot # 34 – 1964) Can't Lose
Kent 396	Let Me Love You You're Gonna Miss Me
Kent 403	Beautician Blues I Can Hear My Name (Hot # 82 – 1964)
Kent 415	The Worst Thing in My Life Got 'em Bad
Kent 426	Blue Shadows (R&B #25 & Hot # 97–1965) And Like That
Kent 429	Just A Dream (Dreams) (Why Do Everything Happen to Me, recorded in 1958, and originally released on Kent 301)

Kent 435	Have Mercy Baby Broken Promise
Kent 441	Eyesight to the Blind (R&B #31–1966) Just Like a Woman (Rockin' Twist)
Kent 445	Five Long Years Love Honor and Obey
Kent 447	I Wonder Why Ain't Nobody's Business
Kent 458	Blues Stay Away It's a Mean World (R&B #49 – 1967)
Kent 462	The Jungle (R&B #17 & Hot #94–1967) Long Gone Baby
Kent 467	Treat Me Right (Oh Baby) (Blind Love. Recorded in 1953, and originally released on RPM 395)
Kent 470	Growing Old (Bad Breaks, unissued 1957 recording)
Kent 475	Soul Beat (Powerhouse) Sweet Thing
Kent 510	Shoutin' the Blues Your Fool
Kent 4526	Worried Life (R&B #4 – 1970) (Walking Doctor Bill, originally released on Kent 350)
Kent 4542	That Evil Child (R&B #34 & Hot #97 – 1971) (Tell Me Baby, originally released on Kent 381)
Kent 4566	Poontwangle

Don't Get Around Much Anymore
(with the Tommy Dorsey Orchestra)

B.B. KING / WITH THE DUKE ELLINGTON BAND
Yes Indeed

B.B. KING / WITH THE SOUTHERN CALIFORNIA COMMUNITY CHOIR (CROWN LP 5119)

(Swing Low) Sweet Chariot
Precious Lord
Servant's Prayer
Jesus Give Me Water
I'm Willing to Run All the Way
Save a Seat for Me
I Never Heard a Man
Army of the Lord
I'm Working on the Building
Ole Time Religion

B.B. KING: KING OF THE BLUES (CROWN LP 5167)

(I've) Got A Right to Love My Baby
Good Man Gone Bad
(from Kent 346)
Partin' Time (from Kent 346)
What a Way to Go
Long Nights (The Feeling They Call the Blues) (from Kent 39)
Feel Like a Million
I'll Survive
If I Lost You
You're on Top
I'm King

MY KIND OF BLUES (CROWN LP 5188)

You Done Lost Your Good Thing Now (from Kent 350)
Walking Doctor Bill (from Kent 351)
Fishin' After Me (Catfish Blues) from Kent 351)
Hold That Train (from Kent 358)
Understand (from Kent 358)
Somebody Baby

Mr. Pawnbroker
Driving Wheel
My Own Fault (Baby)
Please Set a Date

EASY LISTENING BLUES (CROWN LP 5286)

Hully Gully (Twist) (from Kent 372)
Easy Listening (Blues) (from Kent 37)
Blues for Me
Slow Walk (Slow Burn)
Shoutin' the Blues (from Kent 510)
Night Long
Confessin'
Don't Touch
Rambler
Walkin'

A HEART FULL OF BLUES (CROWN LP 5309)

Got 'em Bad
I Can't Explain
You're Gonna Miss Me
Troubles Don't Last
The Wrong Road
I Need You Baby
So Many Days
Down Hearted
Strange Things
Your Letter (from Kent 386)

From 1959 to 1961 sessions, released later on compilation albums:

Shotgun Blues
You Shouldn't Have Left
Shake Yours
That's How Much You Mean to Me
Who Can Your Good Man Be
Recession Blues
I Love You
I've Got Papers on You Baby (Do What I Say)
Tomorrow Is Another Day
We Can't Make It
My Silent Prayer
Don't Cry Anymore

Slidin' and Glidin'
Blues with BB
King of Guitar
Jump with BB
38th Street Blues
Feedin' the Rock
Goin' South
Step it Up
Calypso Jazz
Swingin' with Sonny
Blues at Sunrise
Dust My Broom
Going Home
You Won't Listen
Sundown

1962	ABC 10486	Slowly Losing My Mind How Do I Love You
	ABC 10527	How Blues Can You Get (Hot #97–1064) Please Accept My Love
	ABC 10552	Help the Poor (Hot #98 – 1964) I Wouldn't Have It Any Other Way
	ABC 10576	Whole Lotta Lovin' The Hurt
	ABC 10599	Never Trust a Woman (Hot #90 – 1964) Worryin' Blues
	ABC 10616	Please Send Me Someone to Love Stop Leading Me On

MR. BLUES (ABC LP 456)

Young Dreamer
By Myself
Chains of Love
A Mother's Love
Blues at Midnight
Sneaking Around
On My Word of Honor

Tomorrow Night
My Baby's Comin' Home
Guess Who
You Ask Me
I'm Gonna Sit in 'Til You Give In

LIVE AT THE REGAL (ABC LP 509)

Every Day I Have the Blues
Sweet Little Angel
It's My Own Fault
How Blue Can You Get
Please Love Me
You Upset Me Baby
Worry, Worry
Woke Up This Mornin'
You Done Lost Your Good Thing
Help the Poor

Unissued (*) or released later on compilation albums:
That's Wrong Little Mama (*)
Rockin' A While

1965 ABC 10675   Night Owl
                       Tired of Your Jive

ABC 10710   I Need You
                       Never Could Be
                       You

ABC 10724   All Over Again
                       The Things You Put Me Through

CONFESSIN' THE BLUES (ABC LP528)

I'd Rather Drink Muddy Water
Goin' to Chicago Blues
See See Rider
Do You Call That a Buddy
Wee Baby Blues
In The Dark
Confessin' the Blues
I'm Gonna Move to the Outskirts of Town
How Long How Long Blues

| | | Cherry Red |
| | | World of Trouble |

1966   ABC 10766   You're Still a Square
                      Tormented

       ABC 10856   Don't Answer the Door Pt. 1
                            (R&B #2 & Hot #72 – 1966)
                            Don't Answer the Door Pt.2

       ABC 10889   Waitin' on You
                            Night Life

       BluesWay   Think It Over
       (61004)   I Don't Want You Cuttin' off Your Hair

       BluesWay   Sweet Sixteen Pt. 1
       (61012)   Sweet Sixteen Pt. 2

BLUES IS KING (BLUESWAY LP 6001)
      (I'm) Waitin' on You
      Gambler's Blues
      Tired of Your Jive
      Night Life
      Buzz Me
      Don't Answer the Door
      Blind Love
      I Know What You're Putting Down
       Baby Get Lost
      Gonna Keep on Loving You

ABC unissued (*) or released in 1968 on BluesWay LP 6022:
      Goin' Down Slow (*)
      I Done Got Wise
      Meet My Happiness

1966 BLUES ON TOP OF BLUES (BLUESWAY LP 6011)
      Heartbreaker
      Losing Faith in You
      Dance with Me
      That's Wrong, Little Mama
      Having My Say
      I'm Not Wanted Anymore
      Worried Dream

Paying the Cost to Be the Boss
(R&B #10 & Hot #39 – 1968)
Until I Found You
I'm Gonna Do What They Do to Me
(R&B #26 & Hot #74 – 1968)
Raining in My Heart
Now That You've Lost Me

LUCILLE (BLUESWAY LP 6016)

Lucille
You Move Me So
Country Girl
No Money No Luck
I Need Your Love
Rainin' All the Time
I'm With You
Stop Putting the Hurt on Me
Watch Yourself

1968 Get Myself Somebody (BluesWay 61022)
Don't Waste My Time

FILM SCORE: FOR LOVE OF IVY (ABC LP 7)
You Put It on Me
(R&B #25 & Hot #82 – 1968)
The B.B. Jones (Hot #98 – 1968)
Messy but Good

1969 LIVE & WELL (BLUESWAY LP 6031)
I Want You So Bad (R&B #34 – 1969)
Friends
Get off My Back Woman
(R&B #32 & Hot #74 – 1969)
Let's Get Down to Business

Why I Sing the Blues
(R&B #13 & Hot #61 – 1969)
Don't Answer the Door
Just a Little Love
(R&B #15 & Hot # 76 – 1969)
My Mood
Sweet Little Angel
Please Accept My Love

COMPLETELY WELL (BLUESWAY LP 6037)
So Excited
(R&B #14 & Hot #54 – 1970)
No Good
You're Losin' Me
What Happened
Confessin' the Blues
Key to My Kingdom
Cryin' Won't Help You Now
You're Mean
The Thrill Is Gone
(R&B #3 & Hot #15 – 1970)

BluesWay unissued, later released on a compilation album:
Fools Get Wise

BluesWay unissued released the following year on ABC LP 713:
Go Underground

1970 INDIANOLA MISSISSIPPI SEEDS
(ABC LP 713)
Nobody Loves Me but My Mother
You're Still My Woman
Ask Me No Questions
(R&B #18 & Hot #45 – 1971)
Until I'm Dead and Cold
King's Special
Ain't Gonna Worry My Life Anymore
Chains and Things
(R&B #6 & Hot #45 – 1970)
(Go Underground, from the 1969
'Live & Well' session)
Hummingbird
(R&B #25 & Hot #48 – 1970)

LIVE IN COOK COUNTY JAIL (ABC LP 723)
Introduction
Every Day I Have the Blues
How Blues Can You Get
Worry Worry Worry
Medley:
Three O'Clock Blues
Darlin' You Know I Love You

Sweet Sixteen
The Thrill Is Gone
Please Accept my Love

1971 LIVE IN JAPAN (ABC LP 131-2)

Every Day I Have the Blues
How Blues Can You Get
Eyesight to the Blind
Niji Baby
You Are Still My Woman
Chains and Things
Sweet Sixteen
Hummingbird
You Know I Love You
Japanese Boogie
Jamming at Sankei Hall
Hikari No 88

LA. MIDNIGHT (ABC LP743)

I Got Some Help I Don't Need
(R&B #28 & Hot #92 – 1972)
Help the Poor
(R&B #36 & Hot #90 – 1971)
Can't You Hear Me Talking To You
Midnight
Sweet Sixteen
(R&B #37 & Hot #93 – 1972)
(I Believe) I've Been Blue Too Long
Lucille's Granny

IN LONDON (ABC LP 730)

Caldonia
Blue Shadows
Alexis Boogie
We Can't Agree
Ghetto Woman
(R&B #25 & Hot # 68 – 1971)
Wet Haystack
Part-Time Love
The Power of the Blues
Ain't Nobody Home
(R&B #28 & Hot #46 – 1972)

FILM SCORE: MEDICINE BALL CARAVAN
(WARNER BROS. LP 2565)
    Medley: How Blue Can You Get
    Just a Little Love
    Please Send Me Someone to Love

1972 MAR Y SOL FESTIVAL (ATCO LP 2705)
    Why I Sing the Blues

GUESS WHO (ABC LP 759)
    Summer in the City
    Just Can't Please You

    Any Other Way
    You Don't Know Nothing about Love
    Found What I Need
    Neighbourhood Affair
    It Takes a Young Girl
    Better Lovin' Man
    Guess Who
    (R&B #21 & Hot #62 – 1972)
    Shouldn't Have Left Me
    Five Long Years

NEWPORT JAZZ FESTIVAL 1972
(ATLANTIC LP 9028)
    I Need You Baby
    Blue 'n' Boogie
    Please Send Me Someone to Love

1973 TO KNOW YOU IS TO LOVE YOU (ABC LP 794)
    I Like to Live the Love
    (R&B #6 & Hot #28 – 1974)

    Respect Yourself
    Who Are You
    (R&B #27 & Hot #78 – 1974)
    Love
    I Can't Leave
    To Know You Is to Love You
    (R&B #12 & Hot #38 – 1973)
    Oh to Me
    Thank You for Loving the Blues

THE BLUES!!! A REAL SUMMIT MEETING (ACCORD LP 7212)
    Outside Help (I Got Some Help I Don't Need)

1974 FRIENDS (ABC LP 825)

    Friends (R&B #34 – 1975)
    I Got Them Blues
    Baby I'm Yours
    Up at 5.am
    Philadelphia
    (R&B #19 & Hot #64 – 1975)
    When Everything Else Is Gone
    My Song

B.B. KING AND BOBBY BLAND / TOGETHER FOR THE FIRST TIME... LIVE (ABC LP 50190)

    Introduction
    Three O'Clock Blues
    It's My Own Fault
    Driftin' Blues
    That's the Way Love is
    I'm Sorry
    I'll Take Care of You
    Don't Cry No More
    Don't Answer the Door
    Medley:
    Good to Be Back Home
    Driving Wheel
    Rock Me Momma
    Black Night
    Cherry Red
    It's My Own Fault
    Three O'Clock Blues
    Worried Life Blues
    Chains of Love
    Gonna Get Me an Old Woman
    Why I Sing the Blues
    Goin' Down Slow
    I Like to Live the Love

1975 LUCILLE TALKS BACK (ABC LP 898)
    Lucille Talks Back
    Breaking up Somebody's Home

Reconsider Baby
Don't Make Me Pay for His Mistakes
When I'm Wrong (R&B #22 – 1976)
I Know the Price
Have Faith
Everybody Lies a Little

1976   BOBBY BLAND AND B.B. KING TOGETHER
AGAIN...LIVE (ABC-IMPULSE LP 9317)

Let the Good Times Roll
(R&B #20 – 1976)
Medley: Stormy Monday Blues
Strange Things Happen
Feel So Bad
Medley: Mother-in-Law Blues
Mean Old World
Every Day I Have the Blues
Medley: The Thrill Is Gone
I Ain't Gonna Be the First to Cry

1977   KING SIZE (ABC LP 977)

Don't You Lie to Me
I Wonder Why
Medley:
I just Want to Make Love to You
Your Lovin' Turns Me On
Slow and Easy (R&B #88 – 1977)
Got My Mojo Working
Walkin' in the Sun
Mother Fuyer
The Same Love That Made Me Laugh
It's Just a Matter of Time

1978   MIDNIGHT BELIEVER (ABC LP 1061)

When It All Comes Down
Midnight Believer
I Just Can't Leave Your Love Alone
(R&B #90 – 1978)
Hold On
Never Make a Move Too Soon
(R&B #19 – 1978)
A World Full of Strangers
Let Me Make You Cry a Little Longer

1979 TAKE IT HOME (MCA LP 3151)

    Better Not Look Down
    (R&B #30 – 1979)
    Same Old Story
    Happy Birthday Blues
    I've Always Been Lonely
    Second Hand Woman
    Tonight I'm Gonna Make You a Star
    The Beginning of the End
    A Story Everybody Knows
    Take It Home

B.B. KING NOW APPEARING AT OLE MISS (MCA LP 8016)

    Intro: BB King Blues Theme
    Caldonia
    Blues Medley:
    Don't Answer the Door
    You Done Lost Your Good Thing Now
    I Need Love So Bad
    Nobody Loves Me but My Mother
    Hold On
    I Got Some Outside Help (I Don't Really Need)
    Darlin' You Know I Love You
    When I'm Wrong
    The Thrill Is Gone
    Never Make a Move Too Soon
    Three O'Clock in the Morning
    Rock Me Baby
    Guess Who
    I Just Can' Leave Your Love Alone

1980 THERE MUST BE A BETTER WORLD SOMEWHERE (MCA LP 6162)

    Life Ain't Nothing but a Party
    Born Again Human
    There Must Be a Better World Somewhere (R&B #91 – 1981)
    The Victim
    More, More, More
    You're Going with Me

1981 LIVE IN LONDON (CRUSADERS LP 16013)

    Every Day I Have the Blues
    Night Life
    Love the Life I'm Living
    When It All Comes Down (I'll Still Be Around)
    I've Got a Right to Give Up Livin' (All Over Again)
    Encore

THE CRUSADERS AND B.B. KING / ROYAL JAM (MCA LP 2801)
    The Thrill Is Gone
    Better Not Look Down
    Hold On
    Street Life
    I Just Can't Leave Your Love Alone
    Never Make a Move Too Soon

1982 LOVE ME TENDER (MCA LP 5307)

    One of Those Nights
    Love Me Tender
    Don't Change on Me
    (I'd Be) A Legend in My Time
    You've Always Got the Blues
    Time Is a Thief
    A World I Never Made
    Night Life
    Please Send Me Someone to Love
    You and Me, Me and You
    Since I Met You Baby

BLUES 'N' JAZZ

    Inflation Blues
    Broken Heart
    Sell My Monkey
    Heed My Warning
    Teardrops from My Eyes
    Rainbow Riot
    Darlin' You Know I Love You
    Make Love to Me
    I Can't Let You Go

Unissued, released later on compilation albums:

          Play with Your Poodle
          Make Love to Me (Rehearsal)

1983 LIVE FROM MIDERN, CANNES, FRANCE (KOOL JAZZ LP 26001)
          The Thrill Is Gone
          Guess Who
          Payin' the Cost to Be the Boss
          Jam Session

      FILM SCORE: THE KING OF COMEDY (WARNER BROS LP 23765)
          'Aint Nobody's Bizness If I Do

1984 SIX SILVER STRINGS (MCA CD 5616)
          Six Silver Strings
          Big Boss Man (R&B #'62 – 1985)
          Memory Lane
          My Guitar Sings the Blues
          Double Trouble

1985 FILM SCORE: INTO THE NIGHT (MCA LP 5561)
          Into the Night (R&B #15 – 1985)
          My Lucille
          In the Midnight Hour
          Enter Shaheen

1986 FILM SCORE: THE COLOR OF MONEY (MCA LP 6189)
          Standing on the Edge of Love

1987 GROVER WASHINGTON, JR., & B.B. KING / STRAWBERRY MOON (CBS LP 450464)

      U2 AND B.B. KING / RATTLE AND HUM (ISLAND LP 303400)
          When Love Comes to Town
          (Hot # 68 – 1989)

      FILM SCORE: STORMY MONDAY (VIRGIN LP 2537)
          Stormy Monday
          The Thrill Is Gone

1988   RAY CHARLES AND B.B. KING / JUST BETWEEN
       US   (COLUMBIA CD 40703)
       Nothing Like a Hundred Miles

1988   KING OF THE BLUES (MCA CD 42183)

   Drowning in the Sea of Love
   Can't Get Enough
   Standing on the Edge
   Go On
   Let's Straighten It Out
   Change in Your Lovin'
   Undercover Man
   Lay Another Log on the Fire
   Business With My Baby Tonight
   Take Off Your Shoes

       LIVE AT SAN QUENTIN (MCA 6455)

   B.B. Intro
   Let the Good Times Roll
   Every Day I Have the Blues
   Whole Lotta Loving
   Sweet Little Angel
   Never Make a Move Too Soon
   Into the Night
   Ain't Nobody's Bizness
   The Thrill Is Gone
   Peace to the World
   Nobody Loves Me but My Mother
   Sweet Sixteen
   Rock Me Baby

       B.B. KING AND LEE ATWATER / RED HOT AND
       BLUES (CURB CD 77264)
          Te-Ni-Nee-Ni-Nu
          Bad Boy
          Buzz Me
          Knock on Wood
          Life Is Like a Game
          Red Hot and Blue

1990   RANDY TRAVIS AND B.B. KING / HEROES AND
       FRIENDS (Warner Bros. CD 9 26310)
          Waiting on the Light to Change

BONNIE RAITT AND B.B. KING / AIR AMERICA
(MCA 106770

    Right Time, Wrong Place

B.B. KING AND SONS LIVE (VICTOR CD 103)

    Theme of Unusual – Blue Monk
    Sweet Little Angel
    How Blue Can You Get
    Paying the Cost to Be the Boss
    Guess Who
    Double Deals
    Everything Need Love
    Let the Good Times Roll
    Feelin' Fine
    The Thrill is Gone
    Caldonia
    Darlin' You Know I Love You

LIVE AT THE APOLLO (MCA CD 09637)

    When Love Comes to Town
    Sweet Sixteen
    The Thrill is Gone
    Ain't Nobody's Bizness
    Paying the Cost to Be the Boss
    All Over Again
    Night Life
    Since I Met You Baby
    Guess Who
    Peace to the World

1991 THERE IS ALWAYS ONE MORE TIME (MCA CD 10295)

    I'm Moving On
    Back in L.A.
    The Blues Come Over Me
    (R&B #63 – 1992)
    Fool Me Once
    The Low-down
    Mean and Evil
    Something Up My Sleeve
    Roll, Roll, Roll
    There Is Always One More Time

GARY MOORE AND B.B. KING / AFTER HOURS)
(VIRGIN CD 234)
        Since I Met You Baby

GARY BURTON AND FRIENDS, INC. B.B. KING / SIX
PACK (GRP CD 96852)
        Double Guatemala
        Six Pack

BRANFORD MARSALIS AND B.B. KING / I HEARD
YOU TWICE THE FIRST TIME (Columbia CD 472169)
        B.B.'s Blues

1992   BLUES SUMMIT (MCA 10710)

Playin' with My Friends
(with Robert Cray)
Since I Met You Baby
(with Katie Webster)
I Pity the Fool (with Buddy Guy)
You Shook Me (with John Lee Hooker)
Something You Got
(with Koko Taylor)
There's Something on Your Mind
(with Etta James)
Little by Little (with Lowell Fulson)
Call It Stormy Monday
(with Albert Collins)
You're the Boss (with Ruth Brown)
We're Gonna Make it
 (with Irma Thomas)
I Gotta Move Out of This
Neighborhood
Nobody Loves Me but My Mother
Everybody's Had the Blues
(with Joe Louis Walker)

GARY MOORE AND B.B. KING / STILL GOT THE
BLUES   (VIRGIN 921 472)
        The Thrill Is Gone

1993 DIANE SCHUUR AND B.B. KING / HEART TO HEART (GRP 97722)

No One Ever Tells You
I Can't Stop Loving You
You Don't Know Me
It Had to Be You
All My Eggs in One Basket
Glory of Love
Try a Little Tenderness
Spirit in the Dark
Freedom
At Last
They Can't Take That Away from Me

1994 A TRIBUTE TO STEVIE RAY VAUGHAN (EPIC 485 067-2)
Telephone Song

1997 DEUCES WILD (11711)

If You Love Me
The Thrill Is Gone
Rock Me Baby
Please Send Me Someone to Love
Baby I Love You
Ain't Nobody Home
There Must Be a Better World Somewhere
Confessin' the Blues
Paying the Cost to Be the Boss
Dangerous Mood
Keep It Coming
Cryin' Won't Help You Babe
Night Life

1997 HIS BEST – THE ELECTRIC B.B. KING (MCD 11767)

Tired of Your Jive
Don't Answer the Door
The B.B. Jones
All over Again
Paying the Cost to Be the Boss
Think It Over

I Done Got Wise
Meet My Happiness
Sweet Sixteen
You Put It on Me
I Don't Want You Cutting off Your Hair

1998 BLUES ON THE BAYOU (MCD 11879)

Blues Boys Tune
Bad Case of Love
I'll Survive
Mean Old World
Blues Man
Broken Promise
Darlin' What Happened
Shake It Up and Go
Blues We Like
Good Man Gone Bad
If I Lost You
Tell Me Baby
I Got Some Outside Help I Don't Need
Blues in G
If That Ain't It I Quit

1999 HIS DEFINITIVE GREATEST HITS (5473402)

DISC ONE:
The Thrill Is Gone
Paying the Cost to Be the Boss
Don't Answer the Door (Parts 1 & 2)
I Like to Live the Love
How Blue Can You Get
Why I Sing the Blues
Chains and Things
To Know You Is to Love You
When Love Comes to Town (7" Edit and Mix)
Playin' With My Friends
Never Make Your Move Too Soon
Better Not Look Down
There Must Be a Better World Somewhere

Hummingbird
Everyday I Have the Blues (Live)
Sweet Little Angel (Live)

DISC TWO:
Help the Poor
So Excited
Broken Heart
Ghetto Woman
Ain't Nobody Home
Darlin' You Know I Love You
In the Midnight Hour
Into the Night
My Lucille
The Blues Come over Me
Since I Met You Baby
I'm Moving On
Let the Good Times Roll (Live)
Woke up This Mornin' (Live)
Three O'Clock Blues (Live)
Please Love Me (Live)
Caldonia (Live)
Rock Me Baby (Live)

1999 LET THE GOOD TIMES ROLL (112 042)

Ain't Nobody Here But Us Chickens
Is You Is or Is You Ain't My Baby?
Beware, Brother, Beware
Somebody Done Changed the Lock on My Door
Ain't That Just Like a Woman
Choo Choo Ch'boogie
Buzz Me - King, B.B.
Early in the Mornin'
I'm Gonna Move to the Outskirts of Town
Jack, You're Dead!
Knock Me a Kiss
Let the Good Times Roll
Caldonia
It's a Great, Great Pleasure
Rusty Dusty Blues (Mama Mama Blues)

Sure Had a Wonderful Time Last Night
Saturday Night Fish Fry
Nobody Knows You When You're Down and Out

1999 THE RPM HITS 1951-1957 (ACE CDCHD712)
Three O' Clock Blues
Please Love Me
You Know I Love You
Woke Up This Morning
Story From My Heart & Soul
Please Hurry Me
Bad Luck
You Upset Me Baby
Whole Lotta Love
Every Day (I Have The Blues)
Sneakin' Around
Ten Long Years
Cryin' Won't Help You
I Want To Get Married
Sweet Little Angel
Troubles, Troubles, Troubles
I Need You So Bad
I Wonder
Be Careful With A Fool
(I'm Gonna) Quit My Baby
On My Word Of Honor
I'm Cracking Up Over You
Shut Your Mouth
Did You Ever Love A Woman
Blind Love
When My Heart Beats Like A Hammer

2000 MAKIN' LOVE IS GOOD FOR YOU (112 241)
I Got to Leave This Woman
Since I Fell for You
I Know
Peace of Mind
Monday Woman
Ain't Nobody Like My Baby
Makin' Love Is Good for You

Don't Go No Farther
Actions Speak Louder Than Words
What You Bet
You're on Top
Too Good to You Baby
I'm in the Wrong Business
She's My Baby

2000 THE BEST OF THE KENT SINGLES 1958-1971

Why Does Everything Happen To Me
Days Of Old
You've Been An Angel
Please Accept My Love
Sugar Mama
Mean Ole Frisco
Sweet Sixteen (Parts 1 And 2)
I've Got A Right To Love My Baby
Partin' Time
Walkin' Dr. Bill
Peace Of Mind
Someday
My Sometime Baby
Gonna Miss You Around Here
My Reward

Rock Me Baby
Beautician Blues
Blue Shadows
Eyesight To The Blind
Five Long Years
It's A Mean World
The Jungle
Worry, Worry, Worry
Your Fool
The Evil Child

2000 RIDING WITH THE KING (47612)

Riding With the King
Ten Long Years
Key to the Highway
Marry You
Three O'Clock Blues
Help the Poor

I Wanna Be
Worried Life Blues
Days of Old
When My Heart Beats Like a Hammer
Hold on! I'm Comin'
Come Rain or Come Shine

2001 HERE & THERE: THE UNCOLLECTED B.B KING (556 307)

Caught A Touch Of Your Love - Grover Washington, Jr. (featuring B.B. King)
Monday Morning Blues (from Garfield: Am I Cool Or What? Soundtrack)
All You Ever Give Me Is The Blues (Previously Unreleased in U.S.)
Frosty (with Albert Collins)
T'ain't Nobody's Bizness (If I Do) (from The King Of Comedy Soundtrack)
Six Pack (with Gary Burton)
Three O 'Clock Blues (with Jimmy Smith) (Previously Unreleased Version)
Yes Man (Previously Unreleased)
The Thrill Is Gone (with Willie Nelson)
Get You Next To Me (with Arthur Adams)
Stormy Monday Blues (with The GRP All Star Big Band)

2001 A CHRISTMAS CELEBRATION OF HOPE (112 756)

Please Come Home For Christmas
Lonesome Christmas
Back Door Santa
Christmas In Heaven
I'll Be Home For Christmas
To Someone That I Love
Christmas Celebration

What A Wonderful World
Christmas Love
Blue Decorations
Christmas Comes But Once A Year
Bringing In A Brand New Year
Auld Lang Syne

2002   B.B. KING / THE MODERN RECORDINGS 1950-51 (ACE CDCHM2 835)

CD ONE:
Mistreated Woman (alt)
Mistreated Woman
B. B. Boogie
B. B. Boogie (LP version)
The Other Night Blues (LP version)
The Other Night Blues
The Other Night Blues (alt)
Walkin' And Cryin'
Walkin' And Cryin' (alt)
Walkin' And Cryin' (alt)
My Baby's Gone
Don't You Want A Man Like Me (alt)
Don't You Want A Man Like Me
Questionnaire Blues
B. B. Blues (incomplete take)
B. B. Blues (alt)
B. B. Blues

CD TWO:
A New Way of Driving
Fine Lookin' Woman (alt)
Fine Lookin' Woman
Fine Lookin' Woman (alt)
Shake It Up And Go
She's Dynamite
She's A Mean Woman (alt)
She's A Mean Woman
Hard Workin' Woman
Hard Workin' Woman (alt)
Pray For You
Pray For You (alt)
3 O'Clock Blues
That Ain't The Way To Do It

That Ain't The Way To Do It (alt)
She Don't Move Me No More

2003 REFLECTIONS (MCAB000053202)

2003 MARTIN SCORSESE PRESENTS: THE BLUES 'BB KING' (B0000A0VA5)

2005 ULTIMATE COLLECTION (GEFB000355402)

2005 80 (9885355)

2008 LIVE (GEFFEN)

2008 LIVE AT THE BBC (UNIVERSAL / ISLAND)

2008 ONE KIND FAVOR (GEFFEN)

2012 THE LIFE OF RILEY SOUNDTRACK (UNIVERSAL)

2012 LIVE AT THE ROYAL ALBERT HALL 2011 (Commercial Marketing)

2012 LADIES AND GENTLEMEN... MR BB KING BOX SET (Universal Music) (Released simultaneously as a 4 CD & 10 CD box set)

2015 THE COMPLETE SINGLES AS & BS 1949-62 BOX SET (Acrobat)

2015 UNITED WESTERN RECORDERS, HOLLYWOOD LA, OCTOBER 1ST 1972 (Hi Hat)

2015 THE COMPLETE RECORDINGS 1949-1962 (6 Cd) (Enlightenment Series)

Vintage German tour poster from the 1970's

Vintage posters and adverts for some of B.B.'s many concerts around the world

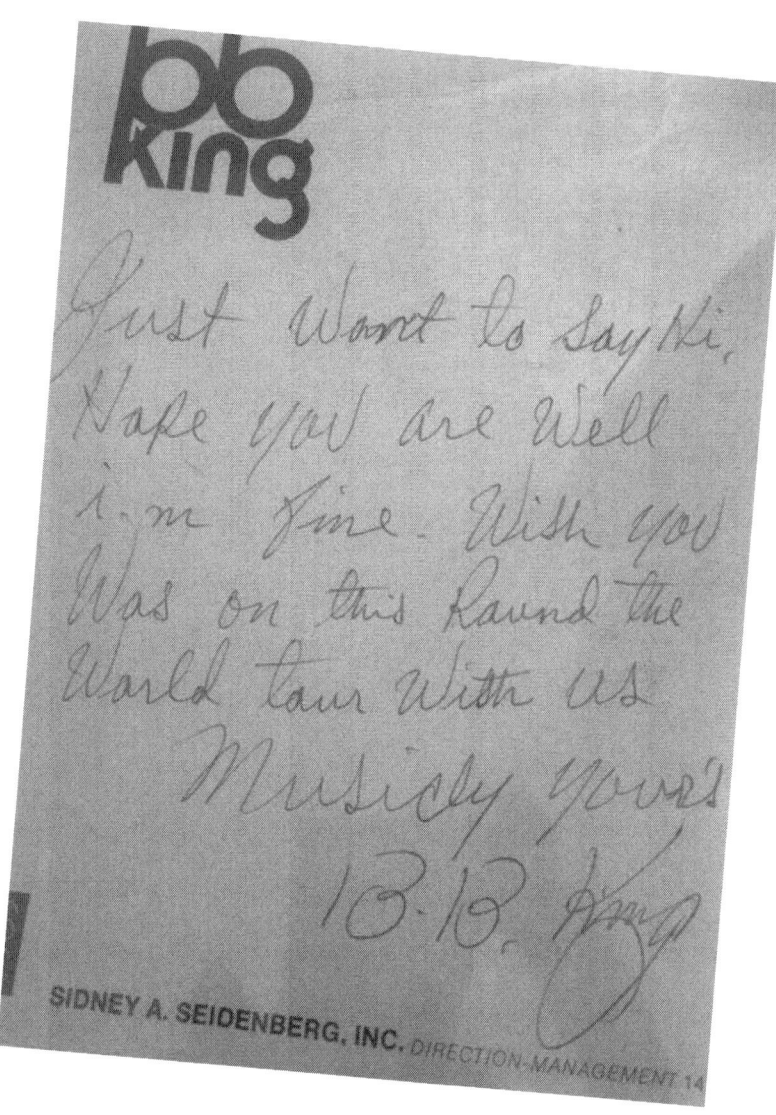

Letter from B.B. (Collection of Richard Booth)

REFERENCES

SELECTED BIBLIOGRAPHY

Books:

Sebastian Danchin - 'Blues Boy' The Life and Music of B.B. King
University Press of Mississippi 1998
ISBN 1-57806-017-6

Galen Gart - 'First Pressings Vol.4' 1954 Ed.
Milford NH Big Nickel 1990

Alan Govenar - 'Meeting The Blues'
Dallas Taylor Publishing Company 1988

Michael Haralambos - 'Right On: From Blues to Soul in Black America'
London Eddison 1974

B.B. King - 'Blues All Around Me' The Autobiography
Hodder & Stoughton / Sceptre Books 1997
ISBN 0340 674806

Joe Nazel -'B.B. King' King of the Blues
Melrose Square 1998
ISBN 0-87067-792-6

Charles Sawyer -'The Arrival of B.B. King'
ADA Capo Press 1980
ISBN 0-306-80169-8

B.B King / Dick Waterman

'B.B King Treasures'
Virgin Books 2005
ISBN 1852272740

Video / DVD / Blu-ray:

B.B. King: Live in Africa: 1974 (2000)
B.B. King: Live at Nicks (1983)
B.B. King: Live at the Apollo (1990)
The Jazz Channel Presents B.B. King (2001)
B.B. King: Blues Master (1995)
The Montreux Dream and B.B. King Workshop (2001)
B.B. King: Sweet 16 (2003)
Let the Good Times Roll (2004)
Joan Baez - B.B. King - I Shall Be Released (2006)
B.B. King: Standing Room Only (2007)
B.B. King Soundstage Live (2007)
B.B. King: at Sing Sing Prison (2008)
B.B. King: Live (2008)
Live In Africa '74 (2009)
Live at Montreux 1993 (2009)
Live at the Royal Albert Hall (2011)
B.B. King: The Life of Riley (2012)
Live By Request (2014)

Websites:

www.bbking.com
www.bluesboyking.com

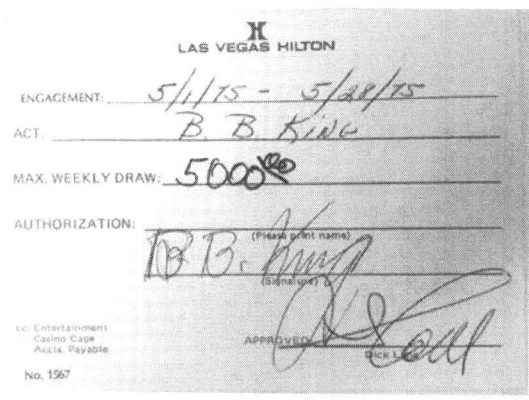

B.B.'s Hilton Hotel Engagement Fee, 1975.
(Collection of Richard Booth)

NOTES

The following extracts used from various books on B.B. King:

Chapter One: In the beginning...

1. Joe Nazel 'King of the Blues' pg. 62/63
2. Sebastian Danchin 'Blues Boy King' pg. 3
3. Sebastian Danchin 'Blues Boy King' pg. 7
4. Sebastian Danchin 'Blues Boy King' pg. 8
5. Sebastian Danchin 'Blues Boy King' pg. 9
6. Joe Nazel 'King of the Blues' pg. 61

Chapter Two: Arrival at Beale Street

7. Joe Nazel 'King of the Blues' pg. 114
8. Joe Nazel 'King of the Blues' pg. 114
9. Joe Nazel 'King of the Blues' pp. 114/115
10. Joe Nazel 'King of the Blues' pp. 115
11. Joe Nazel 'King of the Blues' pp. 114/115
12. Sebastian Danchin 'Blues Boy King' pg. 23
13. Sebastian Danchin 'Blues Boy King' pg. 24
14. Dance 'Interview with B.B. King' pg. 9
15. B.B. King 'Blues All Around Me' pg. 125
16. B.B. King 'Blues All Around Me' pg. 126
17. B.B. King 'Blues All Around Me' pg. 126

Chapter Three: Creating the King

18. Sebastian Danchin 'Blues Boy' pg. 32
19. Sebastian Danchin 'Blues Boy' pp. 33/34
20. Leroy Bonner 'King of the One Nighters'" (Source Unknown (1957) Reprinted in Blues Unlimited 127 Nov/Dec 1977 pg.18
21. Sebastian Danchin Interview with B.B. King Oct 13, 1982

22. B.B. King pg. 14
23. Sebastian Danchin 'Blues Boy' pg. 40
24. Wheeler 'Playing the Guitar is Like Telling the Truth' pg. 63
25. Sebastian Danchin 'Blues Boy' pg. 43\44
26. Sebastian Danchin 'Blues Boy' pg. 44
27. Sebastian Danchin 'Blues Boy' pg. 44
28. Sebastian Danchin 'Blues Boy' pg. 48
29. Billboard (Dec 1954) in First Pressings Vol.4 1954 ed. Galen Gart (Milford NH Big Nickel, 1990 pg. 128)
30. Tri-State Defender (Dec 22nd 1956)

Chapter Four: The Blues is Dying

31. B.B. King 'Blues All Around Me'
32. B.B. King 'Blues All Around Me' pg.197
33. B.B. King 'Blues All Around Me' pg. 204
34. Sebastian Danchin 'Blues Boy' pg.73
35. Alan Govenar 'Meeting The Blues' Dallas Taylor Publishing Company 1988 pg. 95-96
36. 'Rebirth of the Blues' Newsweek May 26th 1969 pg. 84
37. Shaw 'Honkers and Shouters' pg. 521
38. Govenar 'Meeting the Blues' pg. 97
39. Sebastian Danchin 'Blues Boy' pg. 81

Chapter Five: King Worldwide

40. Joe Nazel 'King of the Blues' pg.172
41. Wheeler 'Playing the guitar is like telling the truth' pg. 82
42. Michael Haralambos 'Right on: From Blues to Soul in black America' London Eddison 1974 pg. 58
43. Charles Sawyer 'The Arrival of B.B. King' pg. 22
44. Sebastian Danchin 'Blues Boy' pg. 96

Chapter Six: Returning Home

45. Joe Nazel 'B.B. King: King of the Blues' pg. 181

46. Joe Nazel 'B.B. King: King of the Blues' pg. 182
47. Joe Nazel 'B.B. King: King of the Blues' pg. 185
48. B.B. King 'Blues All Around Me' pg.
49. Joe Nazel 'B.B. King: King of the Blues' pp. 185-186
50. B.B. King 'Bridgewater Hall, Manchester England 3rd July 2001'
51. Joe Nazel 'BB King: King of the Blues' pg. 187
52. BB King 'Blues All Around Me' pg. 187
53. BB King 'Blues All Around Me' pg. 274
54. BB King 'Blues All Around Me' pg. 276
55. BB King 'Blues All Around Me' pg. 277
56. Obrecht 'Memphis and the Early Years' pg. 35

Chapter Seven: Meeting BB King

57. BB King 'Blues All Around Me' pg. 279
58. BB King 'Blues All Around Me' pg. 280
59. BB King 'Blues All Around Me' pg. 281
60. BB King 'Blues All Around Me' pg. 282
61. Richard Booth 'Interview with BB King' 3rd July 2001, Manchester, England

Chapter Eight: Later Years

62. Quote from B.B. King Spokesperson
63. Quote from Hamish Anderson via his Twitter account, April 2014

Chapter Nine: Two White Horses...

64. Reverend Herron Wilson, B.B. King's funeral service May 31, 2015
65. Stevie Wonder audio recording, B.B. King's funeral service May 31, 2015
66. Phil Bryant, Mississippi Governor, B.B. King's funeral service May 31, 2015
67. Tony Coleman, Bell Grove Baptist Church, Indianola,

May 31, 2015
68. Bill Clinton written tribute, B.B. King's funeral service May 31, 2015
69. B.B. King talking to Allan Hammons
70. Allan Hammons
71. Wanda Clark, Mississippi Blues Trail
72. B.B. King Minister for burial service
73. Darwin May, May 31, 2015

Chapter Eleven: Tributes to B.B. With Love

74. "Fans pay last respects to B.B. King in Las Vegas", David Herera; Las Vegas Review Journal May 22, 115 http/ www.reviewjournal.com/entertainment/music/fans-pay-last-respects-bb-king-las-vegas (photo by David Becker)

75. "More Cheers Than Tears"; Fox 411 http://www.foxnews.com/entertainment/2015/05/24/bb-king-memorial-more-cheers-than-tears-in-las-vegas/

76. "More Cheers Than Tears"; Fox 411 http://www.foxnews.com/entertainment/2015/05/24/bb-king-memorial-more-cheers-than-tears-in-las-vegas/

77. "More Cheers Than Tears"; Fox 411 http://www.foxnews.com/entertainment/2015/05/24/bb-king-memorial-more-cheers-than-tears-in-las-vegas/

Chapter Thirteen: Lucille

Various references from 'Guitarist Presents B.B. King', 2011

Tour itineraries and luggage tags during the 2000 World Tour

B.B. waves farewell to his fans during the UK tour 2011

LIST OF ILLUSTRATIONS

All relevant copyright acknowledged by the original photographers where possible.

1. Stanley Abernathy and the author (Collection of Richard Booth)
2. Stanley Abernathy, B.B. King and Jesse Jackson (Collection of Stanley Abernathy)
3. B.B. King 1950's sepia photo, signed by B.B. backstage at the Royal Albert Hall, London, 2011. (Collection of Richard Booth)
4. Signed tour programme from B.B. (Collection of Richard Booth)
5. Signed photo from B.B to the author (Collection of Richard Booth)
6. Concert tickets and guitar pick from 1969 (Collection of Richard Booth)
7. Riley B. King's first home (Courtesy of Charles Sawyer)
8. Beale and Second Street (Courtesy of Memphis and Shelby County Room, Memphis Public Library & Information Center)
9. "Bee Bee Jeebies' WIDA newspaper article (Collection of B.B. King)
10. 'Wheelin' on Beale': Signed book to B.B. by Louis Cantor (Collection of Richard Booth)
11. B.B. King Gibson Lucille (Collection of Richard Booth)
12. With B.B. backstage during the 2006 UK tour and my signed Lucille (Collection of Richard Booth)
13. Very early B.B. King and his orchestra photo (Collection of Richard Booth)

14. Very early BB autograph, inscribed with song title 'You Upset Me' (Collection of Richard Booth)

15. B.B. King and Bill Harvey & Orchestra poster (Texas Music Collection)

16. B.B King playing Lucille (Jas Obrecht Music Archive)

17. B.B King playing Lucille (Collection of B.B. King)

18. Rolling Stones and B.B. King concert poster

19. B.B. King Biggest New Star Award 1946 (Collection of B.B. King)

20. B.B. King's Playboy Music Poll Hall of Fame Award 1992 (Collection of Richard Booth)

21. B.B. King passes and badges (Collection of Richard Booth)

22. Letter from B.B. King (Collection of Richard Booth)

23. UK fan club and website flyers for bluesboyking.com throughout the years (Collection of Richard Booth)

24. B.B. King live at the Bridgewater Hall, Manchester, England July 3, 2001 (Photo: Richard Booth)

25. B.B. King live at the Bridgewater Hall, Manchester, England July 3, 2001 (Photo: Richard Booth)

26. B.B. King live at the Bridgewater Hall, Manchester, England July 3, 2001 (Photo: Richard Booth)

27. B.B. King on stage (André Hobus Photo Library)

28. B.B. and the author at his hotel after his show in Manchester, England, April 1999 (Collection of Richard Booth)

29. B.B. King Worldwide: Passes and Tickets (Collection of Richard Booth)

30. B.B. and the author in his dressing room, backstage at the Bridgewater Hall, Manchester, England July 3, 2001(Collection of Richard Booth)

31. B.B. King Concert tickets, 2006 (Collection of Richard Booth)

32. B.B. King Tour Laminate (Collection of Richard Booth)

33. B.B. King Tour flyer for the Farewell Tour March/April 2006

34. B.B. and the author backstage during the 2006 UK tour (Collection of Richard Booth)

35. Slash, B.B., Ronnie Wood, Royal Albert Hall, June 28, 2011 (Photo: Richard Booth)

36. Flyer for the Royal Albert Hall show, June 2011 (Collection of Richard Booth)

37. B.B. and the author at the Royal Albert Hall, June 2011 (Collection of Richard Booth)

38. B.B. King Aftershow pass, June 2011 (Collection of Richard Booth)

39. B.B. King Tour laminate, June 2011 (Collection of Richard Booth)

40. B.B. King Concert tickets (Collection of Richard Booth)

41. 'One Kind Favor' album cover

42. B.B. King Beale Street Processional (Photo courtesy of James Wessels)

43. B.B. King Beale Street Processional (Photo courtesy of James Wessels)

44. B.B. King's funeral service at Bell Grove, Indianola (Photo: AAP)

45. B.B. King's final resting place (Photo: Hal Hannaford)

46. Memorial card given out at the public viewing, Memphis, May 2015 (Collection of Richard Booth)

47. Funeral programme given out at Bell Grove Missionary Baptist Church (Collection of Richard Booth)

48. Obituary article in The Enterprise-Tocsin, Thursday May 21, 2015 (Collection of Richard Booth)

49. Funeral programme given out at Bell Grove Missionary Baptist Church (Collection of Richard Booth)

50. B.B. King at the Apollo Theatre, Manchester, June 2011 (Photo: Richard Booth)

51. B.B. King Tribute poster, May 2015

52. B.B. King Tribute flyer, Memphis May 27, 2015 (Collection of B.B. King)

53. B.B. King and Tony Coleman (Collection of Tony Coleman)

54. B.B. King and Tony Coleman at Royal Albert Hall, 2011 (Photo: Richard Booth)

55. B.B. King and Tony Coleman (Collection of Tony Coleman)

56. B.B. and John Mayall (Collection of John Mayall)

57. B.B. and John Mayall (Collection of John Mayall)

58. B.B. King image and John Mayall tribute quote (Photo: John Mayall)

59. B.B. King and John Mayall 2009 UK tour flyer (Collection of Richard Booth)

60. Walter Trout, his son Dylan and B.B. (Photo: Marie Trout)

61. Keb Mo and B.B. (Photo: Charley Gallay/Getty Images for Thelonious Monk Institute)

62. Keb Mo and B.B. (Photo: Charley Gallay/Getty Images for Thelonious Monk Institute)

63. Keb Mo handwritten tribute letter to B.B. King (Photo: Keb Mo)

64. Regi Richards - Girona, Spain during the B.B. King tour (Photo: Regi Richards)

65. Las Vegas Tribute (Photo: Las Vegas Review Journal)

66. B.B. King at the Mirage, Las Vegas

67. Early Clover portrait

68. B.B King Blues Club Sign

69. Leonard King showing his first novel "The Lying Tree" to his beloved grandfather, B.B. King. (photo courtesy of Leonard King)

70. B.B. and his Great Grandson (Photo courtesy of Leonard King)

71. Rita King and her Father (Photo courtesy of Rita King)

72. B.B. King's Grammy Award for 'Riding with the King' 2000 (Collection of B.B. King)

73. B.B. King Handprints and signature at 'Billy Bob's', Fort Worth, Texas, 25/09/04 (Photo: Richard Booth)

74. B.B. King autograph (Collection of Richard Booth)

75. B.B. King WDIA Portrait

76. B.B. in action at the Apollo Theatre, Manchester, June 2011 (Photo: Richard Booth)

77. B.B. in action at the Apollo Theatre, Manchester, June 2011 (Photo: Richard Booth)

78. B.B. and the author in Paris, 2009 (Collection of Richard Booth)

79. Tour laminate for European Tour 2009 (Collection of Richard Booth)

80. B.B.'s guitar pick from Paris show, 2009 (Collection of Richard Booth)

81. Ticket for Paris show, 2009 (Collection of Richard Booth)

82. Signed Lucille guitar from B.B to the author (Collection of Richard Booth)

83. B.B. King with his W.D.I.A guitar (Photo: AP)

84. B.B. King's Gibson Headstock (Photo: Gibson)

85. B.B. King's hand in action with Lucille (Photo: AFP/Getty Images)

86. Gibson Lucille guitar (Photo: Gibson)

87. B.B. King at the 1980 New Orleans Jazz & Heritage Festival (Photo: AP)

88. Technical drawings for B.B. King Lucille Varitone Stereo (Photo: Gibson)

89. B.B. King Guitar picks used throughout the years (Collection of Richard Booth)

90. B.B. King RPM '78 record (Collection of Richard Booth)

91. Indianola Mississippi Seeds Test Pressing record (Collection of Richard Booth)

92. B.B. King RPM '78 record (Collection of Richard Booth)

93. Vintage German tour poster from the 1970's

94. Vintage posters and adverts for some of B.B.'s many concerts around the world

95. Letter from B.B. (Collection of Richard Booth)

96. B.B.'s Hilton Hotel Engagement Fee,1975. (Collection of Richard Booth)

97. Tour itineraries and luggage tags during the 2000 World Tour

98. B.B. waves farewell to his adoring crowd during the UK tour, 2011

99. B.B.'s set list for the Royal Albert Hall show, June 28, 2011

100. B.B. King and the author backstage at the Apollo Theatre Manchester, June 2011 (Collection of Richard Booth)

101. Photo gifted to B.B by the author at Royal Albert Hall, London 2011

102. B.B. King Day at MVSU poster: September 3, 2015

103. B.B. King Museum and Delta Interpretive Center

```
BB KING - LONDON ROYAL ALBERT HALL
BB – KING INTRODUCTION
MANHATTAN BLUES
TWO I SHOOT
I NEED YOU SO
EVERYDAY I HAVE THE BLUES
LET THE GOOD TIMES ROLL
BLUES MAN
KEY TO THE HIGHWAY
SEE THAT MY GAME IS KEPT CLEAN
ALL OVER AGAIN
WHEN LOVE COMES TO TOWN
YOU ARE MY SUNSHINE
DIRTY OLD MAN (INTRO TO RockMe Baby)
ROCK ME BABY
THRILL IS GONE
GUESS WHO
WHEN THE SAINTS GO MARCHIN IN
```

B.B.'s set list for the Royal Albert Hall show, June 28, 2011
(Collection of Richard Booth)

The author and B.B. backstage during the final UK tour in 2011

B.B. King
September 16, 1925 - May 14, 2015

Photo gifted to B.B. at Royal Albert Hall, London 2011
(Collection of B.B. King)

B.B. King Day at MVSU: September 3, 2015

B.B. King Museum and Delta Interpretive Center

The B.B. King Museum is dedicated to celebrating the life and music of this iconic artist, and it is B.B.'s expressed wish that education and community outreach be at the heart of their mission. "We honor him and his legacy by providing educational programs designed to offer young people the kind of hope and opportunity that was not available to Riley B. King in the Mississippi of his youth."

B.B. King Museum and Delta Interpretive Center

400 Second Street, Indianola, MS 38751
Phone: 662-887-9539
Email: **info@bbkingmuseum.org**

Proceeds from the sales of this book will be donated to the B.B. King Museum and Delta Interpretive Center

'bluesboyking.com' website

ABOUT THE AUTHOR

Richard Booth has been involved in the music industry since leaving school in 1988. He produced fanzines for a number of bands and in recent years has run websites and undertaken tour photography for bands. He's had his live photos published in music books and magazines throughout the world.

His love of Blues music led him to a lifelong fascination and appreciation of B.B. King. Because of this devotion, he began producing and running the UK BB King fan club, interacting with fans worldwide and with Mr King himself. This led to the 1999 launch of the UK fan site: bluesboyking.com, which has been in production ever since.

Richard has enjoyed the good fortune and privilege to cover B.B.'s tours across the United Kingdom and Europe, reviewing shows and capturing B.B. in live photos at many shows. The last UK show at the Royal Albert Hall was captured by Richard on film and one of Richard's photos from that show has pride of place on the wall inside the prestigious venue at the famous stage door.

Over the years B.B. and Richard became good friends and this book is a lasting tribute to the King of the Blues and to give thanks for all the many treasured years of music, shows and friendship.

All Rights Reserved
For further information contact: Richard Booth
bluesboyking.com

Printed in Poland
by Amazon Fulfillment
Poland Sp. z o.o., Wrocław